A COAST

A Coast

A novel
by

N. C. ROBERT

BOOKS

Adelaide Books
New York/Lisbon
2018

A COAST
A novel
By N. C. Robert

Copyright © by N. C. Robert
Cover design © 2018 Adelaide Books

Published by Adelaide Books, New York / Lisbon
adelaidebooks.org

Editor-in-Chief
Stevan V. Nikolic

For any information, please address Adelaide Books
at info@adelaidebooks.org
or write to:
Adelaide Books
244 Fifth Ave. Suite D27
New York, NY, 10001

ISBN-10: 1-949180-35-2
ISBN-13: 978-1-949180-35-0

Printed in the United States of America

This is a work of fiction. All people, places, experiences, and events are a
product of the author's imagination. As a work of art, all content should
be viewed as such.

To those who are lost and alone.

Content

PART I

The Way, The Truth, And The Life

My name is Rive Devault—I am lost and alone.

I tried to find God five years ago, thought I did—real great—but damned it all since.

Do you have a five-year-plan? I've heard too much about five-year-plans throughout high school and college. Plans are useful in the nearest worries but irrelevant in the long. I had a plan. In the short, it was life-full, promising, respectable and pious. At this time, I thought I knew Him, thought I knew truth, but now He beats at the core of my graspable heart, a pulling source, stretching down bolts between the electric jabs to a hopefully soul, hopefully someone, hopefully good, hopefully going places, hopefully me. He is the reason for my second go, my second plea: I have been starved by Him—and it must be a call. This land must be the tempting desert. O, creation: let me come.

Do you know Him? Do you believe He exists? Let me tell you now that what you are reading and going to continue to read is in no way a religious text, self-help, dogma, or an attempt of conviction. Here is my blood, from left veins pumping, scribing memories of my being, and that of others, and the rest of you. The World.

Here—the coming journey, from the world's youth, the nine-to-five workers, engineers, professors, nurses, cashiers, Jazz struttin' gays, counsellors, berry pickers, Toronto-buzzers, drummers, receptionists, and concrete-laying slaves. Us all hunting.

The World.

The Everybody.

Because we're trudging through the shit of our fathers sins—sweating from the brow, drooling for that badge-baton-guarded golden egg.

This is a conversation. This is a trade of the thoughts inside our skulls.

Demons brought me to watch my mother choke. Hear, hear! That's a story, isn't? But I'll get there. Because to start, this goes back a bit. To start this.

To start this…

Oh, you are in for it now.

★

Life with a *god* began when I thought to be in love with a girl.

The first day of meeting Kerensa, in ninth-grade, she came to first period and sat in front of me. I tapped her shoulder and said, "Nice jeans."

"Gee, thanks," she replied.

We giggled and teased, ending the conversation with mutual insults and that's when I knew. That same day, I invited myself over to her house. We ate dinner with her parents, watched a hockey game, and wrestled on the couch after they went to bed.

I texted her daily and indulged in our class time together. She'd catch me staring always, so would the teachers. I'm not sure if it was her who birthed my obsessive desire, or if she nurtured a seed. I longed for her, and she would tell me she cared, wanted, and might even love me. But she would date older boys. Not me.

One day (of vigorous texting during class) I told her: *If you like me, prove it—right now. Let's meet in the hall.* I knew she wanted me to be more assertive, confident and physical, like the older boys she loved. We met in the hall, muttered awkward nothings, and I took hold of her shoulders. I kissed her, on the lips.

"Like a grandmother," she said.

It was no kiss.

It was the closest I got to her.

The torture went on for three years.

Graduating year. I was in a bad place, and something had to change. One night, I searched for my Bible and began to read. Ending in tears, kneeling, I pleaded to Him for help, forgiveness and guidance. Seventeen-Me thought a girl would be the answer: a Kerensa-substitute that reciprocated my love. Two weeks later, a Kerensa-Lookalike appeared at church and her older sister sang during worship—the epitome of what some would call a *MILF*. It was soon to be realized that this Lookalike was a girl with a name, my age, and had growth up with me in middle-school. While Lookalike's sister praised Jesus in the background, I watched Lookalike in her graceful dress, grazing her figure up through her hair and down to her thighs, with my eyes. And that is when I knew that Lookalike would do. We dated: movies, dinners, hikes and couch time. But I was in love with Kerensa.

With the coming of Lookalike came a new high for Him. I began reading the Word, praying, and making an effort to grow in the faith. I told Lookalike that we should wait to have sex, with intent for marriage. So she sucked me often. I loved those eyes and the places she went with her tongue. We did fun things together with the freedom of my mother's car. But my high for Him was growing. I needed more. I thought of myself above her, as if I desired Him more than she did, wanting a more pious life. And there were decisions to make: whether to graduate and apply for schools, or stay another year. I had dropped down my courses from academic to applied, so my options were limited to colleges instead of universities. I decided to stay another year. Kerensa moved to the west coast with her family. She was gone.

Mother had bugs in her brain. Anxious. Afraid of her child's future. She questioned my future, comfort and status. I was accepted for a social work program at the local college. The choice was mine. But my soul was changing. Life appeared full and lush, all leading to His glory, and no pain in sight. My feet were in step, as they say, "Your walk with Christ." So, I prayed, and preached to my peers. I stopped drinking at parties. All meaning was found in Him. But my feelings toward Lookalike were depleting.

One day, a new youth pastor at the church introduced himself to the congregation. As he talked about his life, family, experience and credentials, I had (what I would call at the time) a spiritual experience. He was in his late twenties, with a beautiful wife, and had joy on his face. His schooling was done at a Bible College called *Servant Steps*.

Something in my mind and soul told me that I wanted to be a *man-of-god* like him. And that was it: ministry was my calling. I stood up after church, walked out into the parking lot under morning sun, and told my parents my decision for the future. Mother was supportive but frustrated with my constant change of mind and lack of direction. Father was indifferent but supportive at distance. I was accepted for a Bachelor of Theology at *Servant Steps*. Mother made sure, in the meetings with guidance counsellors, that the program would allow me to go on and complete a master's degree later, at a "real" university. The guidance counsellor assured her that many students went on to further education, indeed, at secular, established universities.

"You need your master's," said Mother. Her eyes had dark circles, strained and troubled. Her fingers and hands touched about herself as if something had to be fixed, protected, positioned, or purified. She wanted the best for me: to have things, money, status, success. All these would surely come from attending a secular university and acquiring a master's degree. Right? To walk among the proper. The fitted.

The good.

The future.

That summer before college, Lookalike worked as a camp counselor in the city. I worked at a grocery store. Every week the campers would come on a bus to get supplies, so I would see her. We fought in the isles. I knew she no longer cared for me. I also knew she had feeling for a guy she worked with, and without a doubt, cheated on me. She denied it.

A few weeks before I left for college, to *Servant Steps*, I saw news on Facebook: _____ had died drunk driving on a local road. Many people have died down the side roads of such a small town; the youth love to let out their freedom. There's a road the locals call, "Serpent Road," because of its endless turns and minimal use—young folk live to fly through on drunken nights. But this guy lost control and hit a tree. And so, Lookalike posted pictures on Facebook of them together, with hearts and grand words of loss.

"I knew it. You liked him," I said, in the fish isle, on a Sunday afternoon.

"I did. And I don't give a fuck about you," said Lookalike.

A curious course of events. Sad though. But made me ready to go.

My home is a special place. Spinedune is on the lake, and borders the United States. Hoardip Beach moves five minutes from my house. The night before leaving to college I drove frantic to see Lookalike, in need of clarity. The boulevard was my place of comfort. I looked across the lake, to the lights of the city. But there I sat, in a parking lot, screaming in my car, punching the inside, crying out pathetic. Lookalike sat beside me, a frightened cat. She did not care. It was her time to reject me and it soothed her. She got out of the car, into light rain, and walked away.

"Well, your friend is dead. Fuck you! Look what you've done. All is coming together, isn't it? All is appearing true. You fuckin' bitch," I screamed out the window. O, sobbing me, pathetic, driving in rain. But I would enjoy the lights. I would enjoy my city across the lake.

And so began my path to ministry.

★

My parent's faces.

Road.

Servant Steps.

My pants wore tight, shirts chosen with care, and I listened to Christian-punk-metal music and thought it was all so important. It was a phase of adolescent ignorance where all is new and happy. I thought to be different than the rest of my peers, less sheltered and naïve, before speaking to one of them. When I first walked through the dorm, I met Sean. He wore the same shoes and jeans as me. An opinionated fellah. He played his favorite tunes loud, so everyone heard his soul, like me. One night, Sean took me to a special place of his: a train-track bridge. We walked to the middle where there was a ledge. We sat with a speaker, smoking, listening, and talking about God. The tracks looked out to a parallel bridge going over the river where people in cars went to their places and the sun went down. This happened the first month of college. I stopped talking to Sean, but I would go to that place alone to drink and roam.

That first year, I was studious. I took a lot of psychology, counselling, and theology courses. I clung to each word of my professors, for truth. They inspired me to learn, succeed and dress well. So I tucked in button-ups and used the leather briefcase, that Father bought me for Christmas, to carry my laptop. Pens were in my pockets. I tried to wake up to do things like wash my face, stretch, and eat a breakfast. The routine lasted four days. My usual wake-up was past noon, and I went to bed at 3 a.m.

Here were the times of a special freedom. One that you will feel after it is far gone. Attending a college or university is not a requirement to feel this, but it is this stage of life that delivers it. It is the realm of years when you sit in classes full of peers and friends, dupe through courses, worry about nothing but the pretty girls, work a part-time job, buy junk food and booze, and think no further than a coming weekend or social outing. Those who have felt this will know its precise sense and tone. After it's far gone, you will remember. The weather will stir it about in that deep breath you take, in its cold and hots, and you will say, "Oh spring, oh summer, oh fall, oh winter." Oh, something reminds you of whatever it is. No doubt a people, a place, a doing, a being, which you once had, and never will again, with those same someones, in those same blurred-image forgotten places. And all that living, all that doing, has lost them and detoxified it from your being. You have continued to live. Moved on, grown, pursued, maintained. Endured. The doing and being you are now gathers more of these, and you think you enjoy them the most you can, and will remember them as best you can, but they will join the rest. Gone.

By the end of the year, I overlooked my counselling and psychology courses, preferring the biblical, philosophical, and historical. I began to change. But a counsellor was the plan—Mother's plan, thus my plan—and a master's I would get, a master I would be. But I wanted to drink, so I drank and wrote poetry. I was going to be a damn poet, I thought—famous drunk and true.

I wandered drunk at night, across the picnic tables where students would pray in the sunlight, during the day before lunch, behind the dorms where they did bible studies, across the grass where they tried to throw a Frisbee in the sun—smiling for Jesus, saying, "O, Jesus," telling, "O, Jesus," talking, "O, Jesus." Needing, O, God.

"Fucking answer me," I said, one night walking through a cemetery in the fog. A great place to get high. I roamed the graves, lurking, paranoid, twisting my head too fast. But it was freedom.

My first year of college went like that.

★

My parent's faces.

Road.

I was home for the summer.

I took Mother's car to the lake. It was a cold and windy night, not too bad with the windows down: not much snow. I got out to piss, walked up to the rocks (large, mostly flat, all around the parking lot, down-hill to the water), hopped on and up a few then stopped and poised. Eh, there it was. My first visit, outside, reunited to the sight, sound, smell, and storage of memories. My home.

18

Sucking the lake in my nose, ears pounding off the wind. I shivered out fog from my mouth and looked out, across to the city, left-to-right along its core. All the lights. The United States of American, where dreams could come true, and all the apparent thriving souls lived.

I stared.

So, I would be at home for the summer, where Mother returned from work stomping straight to the top of the basement stairs. I stood in my room upstairs. She would stand downstairs, at the basement door, bitching at Father. Beginning with, "Yeah. Fred? What are you doing?" in her unapproved, unsatisfied and punishing voice. The *yeah*, sassed as if she had defeated him.

She was our scalpel, a critic like no other.

"Why are you on the couch again? What did you do today? Where were you? I called your cellphone three times and you did not answer," she said.

A string of zips and zings that left Father to his day-to-day moans on his chair in the basement. I would wait for the slight pause... and my Father's groan.

"WHAAAAT," he pleaded. "No. Don't start. Why? All you do is complain," he said.

At these points, I was scrunched in a creeped-posture outside my room trying to hear every word. I would pity my father for his sluggish care, but I scorned my mother's words.

Mother itched to keep on, saying, "No. No. Fred. Why are you doing this? You can't come home, watch that stupid T.V., after coming home from a desk job, and do nothing. All you do is sit on your rear-end. You're over-weight, Fred, can't you see it? Everyone sees it."

I was embarrassed for him. For his childlike and vulnerable state, as he was exposed of his humanity.

"Okay," he huffed in a heightened pitch like a wining child, "Yes, yes, I know. Okay, just let me be, I'm tired."

But that was just bait for her—because she worked full-time and was always on her feet.

"OH," she said. "Come. On. Fred."

Because how could he possibly be tired if she could work full-time, get the groceries, cook the meals, clean the house and still have energy for her walk every evening? And the sad squabble went on, concluding with the all-around change of nothing and the slam of a door—my que to pull away from my door, upstairs, where I listened. I inched it closed when there was silence and crept back to the desk in my room. All summer I listened to the constant, dead-on ruckus.

There fight was a long and too-old, torturous, teeth-grinding, hair-pull of a listen. A beating, by two self-chained miserable creatures with no way out or attempt to be free from their minds. A nothing but rattling-out noise like chimps in a cage below me.

They hated each other.

★

My parent's faces.

Road.

Servant Steps.

After the summer at home, drinking with friends, I went with worried Mother and thinking Father to begin my second year.

I felt prepared and connected with God. My frail mother hugged me with discontent and disappointment in her eyes. My father reached out to shake my hand. I hugged them goodbye. They drove away.

In my dorm room (the same as my first year), I turned on my computer: loud music. I put things in place while shouting funny things to my friends across the hall. But I was sad. So I laid in my bed, where the sun warmed my cheek from the slit behind the curtains.

This second year, I felt bad about myself: anxious, twitchy, and immoral. But I also felt tough, life-experienced, and socially intelligent. My desire to drink grew.

My favorite professor, Dr. Ledger Hoops, taught Philosophy. He wore wool sweaters and his pants a few inches above his waist. His glasses clucked against his face when he nodded, saying, "Yes, yes, yes," real fast, which was often. Many students found the course to be in conflict with their beliefs, which to me, was bull-shit. I asked questions and presented my views to the class, thinking my thoughts to be original—like a gavel putting slammed. But my peers just turned back to the front after I finished ranting. And so I knew there were synchronized minds thinking the likes of: *wow, okay buddy*; *umm, no not really*; *just stop talking.* Further into the semester, I contributed less.

When I was not in someone's room making jokes, talking while they worked, participating in theological babble, or playing a video game, I drank in my room. During the night, when most were asleep and I had nothing to keep me distracted, I drank to loud music and wrote lyrics. Drinking and writing began—the two correlated in song and spittle.

There was a hotel across the road with a bar. A friend was pissed about something one night and took me there for a drink. A woman, named Joyce, was working. She was in her late fifties, but it was deceiving because her face was sagged under makeup and her hair was bleached blonde. Straggled hair, long, down her shoulders, arching down and straight across her forehead. No doubt she had been doing that job for years.

"Oh, hello, honey," she said. "What can I getcha'?"

Her eyes held tight and her lips pulled in when she was impatient or seemed to be trying to seduce old dirty men, showing her thoughtless handling of duties and decades of experience. I drank whiskey. There were a few regulars along the bar looking at televisions with sports highlights. Joyce leaned up to me when she wasn't busy (which was most of the time). She made jokes, talked about her daughter, told me to date her, and mocked God and my schooling.

I went there three times a week from there on. I would go and sit at the bar, feeling grown, like one of the regulars with a reputation. I met interesting people that were staying in the hotel for work and business. One guy, called Irish, because he was from Ireland, was in town for six weeks for work. He drank whiskey like water. One night he told me a story: "Ah, other night, them women I say. I was drinkin', out clubbin'. I was fucked. When I left the club, these women start yellin' at me! One grabs her shoe. She starts beatin' on me back. So, I look at her. I say, 'Listen…I've never hit a girl before…'" And he stopped his story there, as everyone around him roared. He smirked, turned back to the bar, and sipped his whiskey.

One night, my school, *Servant* Steps, held a baptism in the pool of that hotel across the road. I felt special and in-the-know, older and more mature, that it was my watering-hole. The pool was right by the bar with a giant window across to see everything on both sides. As it got later, many students left, and some girls from school came to swim and giggle. My friends and I went to bar. I had many drinks while Roy, Scott, and Billy came along. They had one drink and laughed at me running around.

Joyce, the middle-aged sweet heart I learned to love and appreciate after weeks of giving her business, had a smile, joked, and made it known of my regular visits. I was proud and it made me louder as I wandered, throwing my arms around the backs of my stiff, sober friends.

I stripped to my boxers and ran out of the bar, around the other side, to the pool entrance, ready to be seen by the girls. In my boxers, I pranced and stumbled up the ladder of one of those flimsy slides. My body slammed onto its stomach, sliding down, and, just before hitting the water, I heard the voice of one of the pretty gals, screeching, "Oh! My goodness! What the heck?"

I got out, running to the bar window, trying to see the other side, my friends, as I pulled up my boxers into a thong and thrusted my bone-hips into the air of imaginary faces. Everyone (faces I could see) across the window laughed but soon turned back to the bar and continued talking. My excitement descended once I couldn't find my clothes.

I was in the pool area with three fellow Bible College girls who presumably had traditional Christian values, and they had just witnessed their unknown classmate strip to his undies, charge the pool, take a dive, struggle out onto the surface, and thrust his pelvis to the window where people were drinking at a bar. Embarrassed of my skinny self, drying off, the foolishness and shame filled me. I got dressed and scurried back to the bar.

These were the three gorgeous girls at my school. A small school, with a particular mind: relationships were God gifted, ordained; physical intimacy was an honor, a privilege to have when one is committed in promise to another. The three girls were smothered with every guy's eye, including mine. But I was convinced to have permission, because I was attractive and their eyes were on me also. I would see them look over, but wasn't sure if that was bound to happen when I kept staring, or if I had caught them in their interest. They were a year younger, first-year students, and had a certain immaturity about them: too cheerful, optimistic, God-centered, and holy. I had always liked older girls: difficult to draw in, independent, bothered, been let down a few times, and intimidated at the need to feel unconcerned or affected by my interest.

The three pretty girls were too easy. Too confident and aware of their desired selves from the limited options. Too expecting and assumed of their eventual romantic choice with too near of a plan set ahead—these girls needed a good fucking. I grunted frowns at them. But a gift from Him came. A few weeks before Christmas, a new girl arrived.

★

One dinner, as students walked into the tiny dining hall, lined up against the wall, chatting and darting heads around, looking at others with an effort to look good, funny, smart, strong, cute, important, and desired, until the door opened, and in came Kailey. She was pretty. Her petite frame in a little dress, smiling with her head down and eyes wandering as if she knew that her everything was being studied. She lifted her head, adjusted her bra straps and said hello to the last person in line. Kailey had smooth dirty-blonde hair in a not-worked-on style, shadowed eyes giver her sex appeal, tiny breasts, full lips and straight enough teeth. But she was always smiling and laughing. Her sense of humor was rare, a boisterous and fun ego that could make friends with ease, and a precise, genuine care for the good of others. Here was another girl to be wanted. Another reason to get up for breakfast, go to class, and be involved with school activities.

We both had a desire for attention and an outgoing nature made it easy for us to begin talking. We grew a mutual attraction. Each talk was brief, cheeky, hindered and unnatural. It took time to develop a true friendship. But one day I told a girl with half-dyed shaven hair, tattoos and a mistreated unfair past (which had manifest into an obnoxious, ruse and vindictive soul) that I thought Kailey was "sexy, funny and awesome." So, Kailey knew that day.

A shy and shoddy man, I added her on Facebook to initiate conversation since the most we discussed were mutual classes, where we lived, and when one of us was getting a coffee. I started with a "Hey," and after her response, a "How are you?" The girl's floor was upstairs, her room right above mine, so I imaged her typing, if she sat at her desk like me or laid on her bed anticipating my reply, then smiled when it came. She was so near. Walking outside to the dining hall for dinner, I had jitters for the possible timing of her leaving as well. I came through the doors scanning at once. She was there. We looked at one another and away just as fast. I stood in the back of the line with a new excitement, a new girl to possibly love me and another set of moments to feel fulfilled.

On our first date we walked to a coffee shop. I told her everything, an effort to be vulnerable with the hope of its admiration but also the out of egotism. I told her about my adolescent nonsense, daily drinking, love for weed, hate for certain people, and ex-girlfriends.

A few weeks went by and she was my official girlfriend. The first of my time at Bible College. And she had a car. Christmas came and we left for her house to celebrate her sister's, Paige, birthday. I was excited to meet her family and grow close with them. Other people's families were always important to me, because they gave me an example of what seemed to be a normal love and familial care, which I could feel a part of. And it was close to the holidays—good timing.

It has since become a memory that I continue to relive in its vivid look behind, a well-defined sharp sketch making its rare appearance only in the oddest of time. I have few of those memories.

Driving to her house, I asked about her siblings: she had four-year-old twin sisters, two younger brothers by a few years, and her sister, Paige, one year younger. Her father, a pastor, was easy-going, which surprised me. We got along well. Before the got together he had messaged me:

> *Hi.*
>
> *This is Kailey's dad. I see you are one of many that have been chosen by my daughter as a boyfriend. Hopefully this lasts longer than the last one. I hear you're coming over in a few weeks so I thought to tell you that I accept gift cards. Also, there's a real great biker gang that has a bible study at our church. Many would love to do any favors for me if needed. Just thought I'd let you know. See you soon.*

I liked the sense of humor.

We pulled into her family-home driveway. I made sure my shirt was tucked, hair in place and handsome. I took a deep breath and made the fog I could. The instant of entry, the twins stood in their perfect sameness holding hands giggling, asking to play. Wafts, delicious meal, soft Christmas tunes, and the laughs of family in fellowship. The twins ran to their rooms getting toys, around the house, jumping for me to play. Kailey's mother was in the kitchen cooking and calling for her little helpers to come assist in the kitchen, which they happily complied. I wanted to be a holy man, admired, respected, and relied on. I wanted to serve God with a fulfilling job while still receiving a successful wage—to be a complete man. To have a nurturing, pure-hearted wife of natural-beauty and kind eyes. To have children that would become advocates of truth and justice. I was glimpsing into that life.

I wanted it.

But there was a guy named Matt who seemed a better fit. And he had a connection with Kailey before I began dating her. And they still talked daily. He believed himself to have the gift of prophecy and gave Kailey a letter the day before that dinner, which pissed me off.

As we sat down for dinner, I explained to Kailey's dad about Matt and the letter.

"The letter was loaded with bull-shit and fancy talk, trying too hard to sound intelligent and godly,"

But I did not use the word *shit*. Matt had also written that he had a vision with red-flags, which he believed to be a sign that her dating me was a mistake. The father just listened to me rant, saying, "Oh, wow," and, "Oh, really?" We began to eat.

Lovely dinner. The birthday-sister, Paige, brought out the desert she made, a tower of charming cupcakes, each one a crafted-care for us all even though it was her birthday. As we enjoyed them, the brother came home. He had a nerdy, snobbish intellect about him. He said two sentences to me: one mocking me about something trivial I had said. But I did nothing. It was my girlfriend's brother after all, the first meeting, and that's what brothers do to their sister's boy-friend.

We moved into the living room, sipping coffees and cocoa as Paige opened her presents. I sat in a Lazy Boy with one Kailey's twin sisters in each arm. I studied Paige, seeing how similar she was to Kailey: pretty, full of joy, worthy of ad-miration. But I made the odd discovery that she was more appealing as a mate.

The family dog was old and boring, but I dropped to the floor and gave her love. She rolled up for a tummy-rub and I scratched away making dumb sounds with my lips pushed out. Hailey's dad came by.

"Aw, crap. The dog likes you. I guess that's a sign," he said.

Before the night's conclusion, I put a lightbulb in the grandfather's car which put a wrap on what seemed to be a successful evening.

Driving home, Kailey and I brought up each conversation that had occurred throughout the night. We laughed and came to a good conclusion of each one. But there was something crawling in my head.

Without warning, I said, "Why the fuck would Matt give you a letter? Why does he talk to you? Do you still talk to him? You led him on and flirt without knowing! Why do you have to be so flirty? Why the fuck would you still talk to him?" And on and on with no aim or chance for her to reply.

She started crying and said, "Why are you doing this, this was a big deal for me. Do you realize that this was the first time I brought someone home? This was important to me and you are ruining it."

I said nothing the rest of the drive.

Back at school, in the parking lot, I continued. The fight ended with her in my arms, a hug and kiss goodnight, as we walked to our dorm. The first three weeks of our relationship we fought each day, followed by apologies. Always reasons spawning inside my head, digging its way out to be freed. And I let them out without caution or control. I made her cry every day.

One night we drove in her car to a park down the road from the school.

We kissed with passion.

I grasped and rubbed her chest, thighs, up to her neck, the back of her head, pulling my hand through her hair. Took her sweater off, started unbuttoning her jeans, off with her shirt, leaving her just in a bra. I pulled the jeans to her knees massaging her outside. Fog came in the windows. Kissing her neck, I took off her bra and her breasts were pointed so shy and never seen. Licking them, sucking them. She pushed her breaths fierce, and now the fog covered thick all around. I slipped my hand in and entered her. With no coordination, too taken by my fingers, she rubbed me without a clue of her actions outside my pants, just moaning away.

Then I saw a light. A light directed at the car and moving closer. We jolted up. She hurried to throw on her sweater, stuffing her bra beneath the seat. I thought there was nothing to do but sit, facing forward unassuming and innocent. A flashlight poked into the car, searching. I opened the door and said, "Hello."

An officer asked what we were doing and then looked at Kailey.

"Are you here on your on will?" he asked her.

Kailey's eyes darted and her lips quivering, "Yes, yes, yes," she said.

After checking my license, the officer asked why I was in the city if I was from Spinedune, and to that I responded with anger in my voice, saying that I attended school down the road, the girl and were just talking and drinking hot-chocolate, as I lifted a cup.

"Alright," said the officer. "Windows are real fogged up though." He paused. "Just make sure in the future you don't come here past eleven. There's been kidnappings here not that long ago, that's why I came over here." He returned my license and walked away. I shut the door and noticed the speed of my heart.

"O, my God," Kailey said, with a quivered smile. "That was so embarrassing, O, my God."

A week later we broke up. She wouldn't tell me why and refused to meet in person to talk about it. That drove me mad. I hated not having closure or even a reason. I smashed the walls in my room and cursed loud without a care of any ear, seething at the thought of her being too weak to talk in person and break up with me like an adult. I went upstairs to her dorm, but her room was empty. I sat on her bed and waited. Shaking. Stabbing every thought and ending in my head. Hearing her voice, I perked up.

Her face dropped when she saw me.

"Can I talk to you alone," I demanded.

She huffed her willingness. From then on it was begging, pleading and promising being thrown out of my mouth in all directions of the tiny room while she walked around it, away from me as I followed her with my wining voice. Crying, she told me that I had to leave with no care on her face—and the slightest humor found in the joke before her. My crying was a pushed wailing pout and I could feel my strained face muscles and dry eyes. Her friend came and said I had to leave. I said, "Please." Again and again, I pleaded, as I was forced outside the door of the dorm. Her friend shook her head, and Kailey pushed me away with her leg. Trying to close the door, her face bewildered, close to a laugh, she slammed it.

Silent at once. I drove my hands through my hair, clenching. A grunt. I took slow steps down the stairs hoping no one was below, or had been. As far as I knew, it was all unheard. I walked to my room. I sat at my desk. I poured myself a drink.

I spent many days at my desk drinking. Two weeks after Christmas, I was almost over Kailey. I saw her a few times, passing by her on the court yard at lunch, the dining hall each meal, the lecture building, its shop where we got coffee, and the staircase in the dorms where we had stood beneath to kiss goodnight. Each of those paths were crossed, and I was free. She kept walking around with her little dresses and self, choosing to flaunt and shine, free for the taking by another.

Weeks passed, a month. Two.

Now, just bitter of the entire her, at her mention I let out jeers and scorns. Hearing her voice down the hall, I'd burst out, "Oh, fuck," and "Just shut up." When I saw her in a friend's room I'd look in her eyes with a face of strike and violation, leaving without a word for her or my friend. I was on my way to proper health. It was the last month of my second school year.

I drank more than ever.

★

I found another girl.

Vivian.

At a Sunday night soccer league I let out anger and showed off the little skills I had. If fouled by someone, I lashed out with curses and pulled them close by their jersey. The girl, Vivian, was a blonde, not petite, but athletic. A good player, best girl, made smart plays, great passes, scored the occasional goal. When she had the ball I made comments shouted comments about her skill and beauty. She blushed and giggled. I heard her name and searched for her social media. I asked her to meet for dinner with me and some friends.

Drinks in a small group seemed for a good ease into something of a friendship. Friday we would meet. The following Sunday I went to soccer with gel in my hair. Entering the gym, I scanned. She was dressed well, not changed and ready to play, looking stunning. But there was a guy close beside her. I glanced many times and one of them was met with the guy's eyes. He had thick combed hair, strong jaw, well dressed, and wore a shiny smirk as he put his arm around Vivian and stroked her back. An instant thud and a rip in my gut, as if she were mine, being groped by another man. The rest of the night was shit. Back at school, I walked into my room, put down my bag, poured whiskey, and slammed out a message to her: *That was great. Why wouldn't you tell me you had a boyfriend?* She said that the guy was just a friend. It made no sense. I continued questioning. She said that she had no romantic interest in him, but he liked her and was weird, that's why he put his arm around her. It made no sense. I asked if he knew about me. She said he didn't, he must have seen me staring. To that, I became defensive, as if I were a creep from afar. I said a few more words and stopped talking to her until Friday. Our first date.

She walked into the restaurant with jewelry on important places, wearing white soft clothes: golden watch, silver necklace, dark ass-tight jeans. She sat down next to me. Masking her nerves, confident and quick to get through the small talk, she put her hands against my cheeks and said, "My hands are so cold, feel them." I remembered her doing the same to a guy at soccer two weeks prior. She got settled and took off her jacket. I had a beer and made bad jokes, but she laughed and so did my friends. We talked about her childhood home in Ottawa, family, faith, high school, and the future.

I messaged her another day asking if she wanted to come over to the college and hangout. I froze and stared at my computer screen for eight minutes after it showed the message had been read. She went offline. Trying not to let it mean anything—maybe she was building suspense—not coming off desperate or impatient, I said nothing more. The next morning, I awoke angry, seeing no response, and sent numerous question marks. It took five for her to respond. But she did: *Yes.*

It was the day.

I made my bed for the first time since being in college. Most of the guys were on a prayer walk so the dorm was empty. She was to arrive in ten minutes and meet me at the main building. I scurried out of my room, out the building, down the path to the main, watched a car drive away from the parking lot ahead, and I saw a girl. A well-curved, long hair, beauty of a girl, walking slow to me. It was an odd walk to out meeting: thinking of a hug, if I should hug, what I should say, whether she was thinking of a hug, if she wanted it, if she had the thought, and if she was also as riddled over it all. But she waited by the door. I opened the door and reached out for a hug, but she didn't notice. I showed the school grounds for no reason. I could hear myself talk and see myself sweating, adjusting my clothes. Then we went to my room.

"Here it is," I said, with a sweeping arm.

She sat on the edge of the extra bed across from mine. I went to my desk out of habit and safety. She smiled and swayed to the instrumental tunes I began to play, following with her eyes. "What do you want to do?" I asked.

"I don't know. You tell me," said Vivian.

"You don't have to sit over there. You can some sit beside me."

Without hesitation, she did.

The guy from soccer was discussed because I needed answers. She voiced her frustration, showing her emotion for the first time, telling me how frustrating it was because the guy meant nothing, and it was interfering with whatever it was we might become. I made her promise that he was nothing. "Yeah," she said. That was a promise.

But then we arrived on the topic of her past romance. Her first and only love in high school.

"Did you sleep with him?" I asked.

She didn't look in my eyes when she answered. "Yes." She explained how her ex had broken her heart after cheating more than once.

"Why would you go back to him then?" I asked.

"Because I loved him," said Vivian.

Having no right to be, I was crushed.

I told her I had slept with people in the past too.

But at least we were getting to know each other. I looked at her and moved closer. Vivian hid her thoughts and feelings with ease. I had no idea if I had made her jealous, or turned-off by the attempt to get close. She had leaned against the wall and I made about five inches in progress toward her. The talk seemed to have reached its goal. Waiting for some silence, timed with our eyes looking into one another, she must have known, as it came, and I went up by her neck and kissed her. Like playing a part in a film, she sat cross-legged returning it all. I moved down her neck.

Hands got involved, one of hers at my waist, both of mine along her torso. We made-out for twenty-minutes, passionate and lush with peaks of aggression. The time in between fooling around we laughed over randomness and cuddled.

But then it was time for her to leave. I waited as long as I could to stand up. I could feel stickiness in my pants, but I leapt up without a care. Our goodbye, at the doors of the dorms, we embraced and went inside each other with our tongues. Then she left.

I walked to my room. At that point, I was sure of our soon-to-be relationship and her having the title of my girlfriend. But the first and immediate thought was that I would masturbate. No, not to porn. A photo of Vivian.

My second year of college went like that.

★

My parent's faces.

Road.

I sat at home again.

It was summer, and I called Vivian during the nights and walked aimless. The wind drove into me when I stood

screaming at the lake. I made my way up a hill, around forests
and parking lots as we talked about nothing. All that was said
had no end. I condemned her actions and anyone and any-
thing that she spent time with.

The summer went like that.

★

My parent's faces.

Road.

Servant Steps.

It was the start of my third and last year, and I had my
mother's car.

I drove and lit a joint. This was freedom.

The touch of cool from coming fall came through the
windows, tunes loud enough. I hate the worry of work.
Thinking about work. Anything about work is tantalizing
and unwanted, a miserable ache and pain of the future and
its worry. Chains. I fucking hate the chains of worry and ri-
diculousness of giving time to a thing that is never going to
be changed or even slightly budged by that tool: Worry. It is a
waste. But I guess it keeps caution bickering in the mind.

A cigarette in me with the wind and odd rain drops
smacking my face as I bopped and jittered down the highway.
I headed up the City Bridge and towards the rays of light
peeking through in the distance. There were dark clouds,
pleasant, freeing my head, while I thought of the common
waste of cigarettes when you ash them too soon, before every-
thing is burned through and is sucked out the window, to the
world and its natural end.

I flicked, anxious, without ashing anything so I decided
that I would start waiting, and savor the life of a cigarette.
Being in my car with the wind coming through, under the

clouds and the rain was a cherished time—music and a hand out to the wind: In love.

I arrived in the city and picked up Vivian before getting to school. We moved my things in the dorm while people went about campus in that fresh way of a beginning school year. I enjoyed having her with me looking beautiful as if I were better and above because of her presence. Then we got alcohol and looked for a place to park so we could have sex and stay the night.

We got high by the bridge and the train tracks. It was late and I put the seats down in the back and laid out blankets. We crawled into them and shivered up to one another, clothed, smiling with our faces together, and made love.

There was a trail that leads to a dock where people fish and launch kayaks. We stood on it and got high looking at black sky, talking about the coming year and us. It was my last year before making another decision to pursue my master's. It stressed her out to not have finished her own schooling and prolong her degree. We had choices ahead of us. They could have lead anywhere. My plan was to do get my master's as my mother had expected. Vivian envied that my parents were paying for my education. She worked much harder than I did and was diligent in her studies.

Her father, once at dinner, had told me that Vivian was a superior student. He said there were levels of people in this world, and Vivian was in the top. She was an honors student, kind, caring, intuitive, and beautiful. I knew all of those things.

Her father found a picture of me shirtless in a hotel room. It was on Vivian's phone. I called the house one night asking for her and he answered.

"Hello Rive," he said. "I want to meet with you, when you get in town, and have a chat. How does breakfast on Friday morning sound?"

He voice was direct and reproached.

We met for breakfast. I couldn't eat much, too nervous. He asked me what I liked about Vivian and I told him that she was beautiful, smart, different and more interesting than others. He said that she was more than that, and then listed her highlights and achievements. I listened, nodded. There was silence.

"I found a picture the other day," he said. He asked the waitress for a pen and began to write on a napkin. "Alright. In this world there are different things that affect our spirit. Family, substance, sex."—he looked up to my eyes—"and things that live among us—demonic influences." He drew stick figures and explained how, as a man, I was to stay clear of these things, protecting my wife and family. As a man, I was the spiritual leader and influence on my family.

He jabbed the pen on the word *sex*.

"Now, if this is going on, in any way, I am going to hurt you," he said.

His lip quivered. I whimpered that I was sorry, not confirming or denying that I had slept with his daughter. He dropped back in his chair and bopped back forward.

"If this happens again, I am going to hurt you," he said. "She's mine. Do you understand? She is mine."

I could see the heart break in his eyes, that his daughter had been tainted by a young man of such low status and holiness. "Enjoy your breakfast," he said, before getting up and leaving.

That was it.

I had kept that napkin and put it on my desk. There was something exciting and encouraging about the whole meeting. The next day I met with Vivian as a pious man. I told her we had to start to pray together, read the Word together, and stop having sex. That did not last a week.

She got a job at the hotel across the road from my school. I had brought her there one day for lunch and Joyce raved about her beauty, saying she would be a great bartender and make a lot of money. She offered her a job, and Vivian was excited because she loved the idea of working right across the road from me.

The year went on with my usual drinking, grueling at assignments and spending all the time I could with her. I was at the hotel even more. But as the months went on, Vivian complained about the environment, how it hurt her soul because of the foul people coming through. There were many prostitutes that worked in there and would come to the restaurant along with their pimps.

One night, when she was at work, she kept texting me that she was afraid. A guy was their telling her that she could make a lot of money because she was sexy. After hours of harassing her, she told him to fuck off. The guy called her a bitch. And that was that. She quit after two weeks, which was good, because I hated her working there just as much as she did.

It was then two months into the semester, beginning November, and our relationship was horrid. We fought all the time (thinking of it now is keeping my skin tight, cold to my little bones sticking out, I'm drugging, jotting to whiskey, in the place that all of this leads to, and I listen to the tunes that I listened to, often, driving around alone, and with her), because I was always jealous, demanding, condemning or accusing of something that she had done or seemed to have done. I did not trust her. We were still in what seemed like love, and we would get hotels, drink, get high, have sex, sit in the bath drinking wine, but then fight, and I'd scream: *what the fuck; answer me; fuck you; why.*

But I wrote a poem for her one night, drunk off a bottle of wine, and it was the first one I got published. I was spending more time drinking and writing. Poetry became the best form of work and art.

Vivian was not the first girl I wanted to marry, but she was the first that made sense—so in a way, she was. Kerensa had been a high-school obsession, and Lookalike was a high-school sweetheart as well my sexual tool and fulfillment—but Vivian was my love.

Vivian's poem was the first of an intended sculpting, with purpose, from the onset of a pen that had form and fuel, titled, "Held Below":

★

All feel and fear with no giving hand to care.
No, real eyes swell, I swear with tears, none can never cry
When fear is begged but never dies.
And we are all begging.

★

We start this year.
Do you see that strength left me long ago?
Where the life of our love rests
In the arms of time's well known,
To prevent me from talk,
Stopping me the rise of the morning walk.
You have lost my sun.

★

She moves in sounds, patient pains and silent frowns.
She lives in stares, beneath my chin as tears cut air.
She wore my heart at day and soul by night,
Now walks my dreams, soaked by dusk
As my once hand just holds her light.

★

*But now I want to know what makes you shake
And how to hold your heart to blaze goodwill.
Why have you gave and why have you taken?
What keeps you still? Why you would and never will?*

★

*Where will you go?
Know that earth has no end.
And gods toss the sun, while catching the moon,
To bring the day and take the night.
With hands so slow and bruised, on way to death by June.*

★

I gave it to her on a folded page written long-hand before she drove home one night from spending time together in my bed, having sex, at the campus. We were in love and both sure as hell about it. It was a love that had real potential for marriage, although not guaranteed or even probable to be one of good health. A love of innocence, passion, carefree play and careless desire. But plagued: jealousy, lies, habits, control, lust, inconsistent truths.

One evening, a week before Christmas, she called me at three in the morning.

"Can you come and get me," she sobbed.

"What? Where are you? What the fuck? Where did you go?"

There was a staff Christmas party that she had said she would not go to. I didn't like the guys she worked with. There was a guy she worked with who remarked on her looks.

She sobbed and mumbled.

"Vivian! Honestly, where are you? I'll come get you," I said.

"I'm at the party."

"Wow, what the fuck? Are you serious? Alright, what's the address?" I said.

I was more concerned than mad, racing to get my keys, worried for her safety and sickened by the thought of her at a party with hungry men.

"I don't know, I'll text you," she said.

"No just tell me, where are you?"

She hung up.

Then the anger. I ran outside in the snow and cold. I slipped on the ice, slammed to my ass. The gas in my car was on empty, and ice layered the tank shut, so I scraped at it with my key. My mind and body responded as if in emergent state, breathing rapid and dismayed with no chance of opening the tank. I raced on.

I got a text with the address. She was not responding to me, yet she sent multiple messages, asking to hurry, that she needed me, which drove me into a spiritual, intelligible madness. Reaching the house, I was ready to fight—not with her, but any guy who would say the wrong thing or undermine my presence.

A guy answered the door in a calm and casual manner.

"Yeah, she's here," said a guy. He turned and ran up the stairs. "Hey Vivian, there's someone here."

She stumbled down in a tiny dress looking gorgeous.

"What the fuck are you doing?" I demanded.

She mumbled and moved in familiar ways. I was quick to realize her drunk speech and behavior. Her eyes shone red, cooked straight through.

"What the fuck are you doing, you're high, I can tell," I scorned.

"Nothing, let's go." She fumbled to leave.

But I wasn't going anywhere without answers. "No. Fuck you. What the fuck are you doing, Vivian? Tell me the truth." Again and again, I pried. But she verged to a cry with no answer, and that thrusted me into insanity. I shoved her shoulder. Then again.

A guy upstairs, who had been watching, asked what was happening.

I ran up the stairs in wrath and rage, ordering: "What the fuck is going on, and why is my girlfriend calling me crying? Who the fuck are you? Tell me what happened. I swear to God..."

"Nothing man, calm down. I don't know," said one.

"Let's go," I commanded to Vivian. She was embarrassed and tried to calm me down, but I continued. There were four guys and two girls frozen still in a living room, caught in the rage at the center of me, the random lashing-out aimless.

"Why are you looking at me?" asked one of the guys. It was the guy I hated (who flirted and commented on her looks), exactly how I assumed him to look, talk, posture and carry himself. A worm. A fucking creep. Foolish, in my eyes, for stepping to me the way he had.

"Who the fuck are you?" I said. My eyes dug deep, thrusting my words like a knife into his. "I swear to god, I'll fucking beat the shit out you. I'll beat the shit out of all of you."

"Rive, please, stop, let's go," said Vivian.

She staggered at the bottom of the stairs.

No one moved. One guy got close and put his hand on my shoulder. "Nothing happened man, it's all good," he said, attempting to calm me down. "You seem like a good guy, but you're coming in here yelling. Your girlfriend is crying, and you're threatening people you don't even know." His face, and the way he spoke, was respected by me for whatever reason, so I walked down the stairs.

Demanding answers was no use because I did not intend on listening. She was too distraught and dazed. I shoved her again and she almost fell down the stairs to the basement (the look on her face once she got her balance and lifted her head to me, is an infrequent thought of memory, that erupts an impulsive cringe and audible wince in disgust of my behavior. Nauseous shame and heartache for the trembling girl in front of me, so in love, with the man shredding her heart and soul) where I did not relent, and she gave quiet responses of how she had done nothing wrong: she didn't deserve to be punished.

In selfish, pitiful spite, I knew she had not cheated or done anything worth damnation, but I began making her feel guilt and shame for her actions with dramatic claims of pain and sorrow from her harmful actions that prove her lack of love and respect for me and us.

We made our way outside, in string-cold rain.

She shivered bare-foot in her tiny dress and drooping lips until one of the guys came and put his arm around her, saying, "You need to go buddy, its freezing and she has no coat or shoes. Just go, get out of here buddy." He led her inside.

"Yeah, Rive, just go," said Vivian.

I fled to the school and stomped to my room.

I trembled out a sloshing pour of whiskey: quivered it down, with a gag, a rocking back-and-forth in deranged fester on the end of my bed, waiting for the earliest time that I could go to Vivian's house. When I got there, her mother answered the door, frowning, surprised. Vivian was not home. I rambled on about her having gone to a party and calling me drunk in distress to be picked up.

"Well she called earlier this morning, saying she slept over at a coworker's house," said her mother.

Then Vivian's younger sister peeked from behind and smiled. She sat on the stairs and listened. I continued on with my disapprovals and concerns. Her mother signed and rolled her eyes with a few comments of indifference and routine disappointment in another let-down and lie from her eldest daughter. "I'll have her call you when she gets home."

It was six-thirty in the morning when I sped off from her house. I was supposed to go home the next day, but all senses swam in dread and chaos. Without thought, I grabbed what was needed, got in my car, and raced to the highway for home (thanking some god for a joint and cigarettes found in the car). The drive had a soothe once the sun peeked, and the high seeped in my mind, stroking soft paint over the slash and chiseled terror left on the walls in my head.

I was home for the holidays.

Christmas.

The two-week break was a crawling of moaning in agony, pity, and shame of my pathetic being. Fixed, like a gremlin to the cell phone in my hand, despite being set on shunning Vivian until she came to me first, I hoped she would come begging—plea for my love. But it did not come. I was the first to act, when I texted her the day before returning to school: *Why have you not said a word? How are you not begging for my forgiveness?*

Her response: *I am sick, Rive, and everything has been so busy over Christmas, with siblings and family home.*

She took hours to respond, but when she did, the breach of silence brought the flood of messages like an insect crawling and chewing through my mind in a scurry from thought to thought. Her messages were short: *I am sorry, alright?* Her response was telling of her belief that she was free of conviction and blame.

Home made me itch. I was impatient to leave and address my relationship, but I went to the get high and play pool with friends at a bar by the beach. We slandered and joshed our drinks about with our arms around another, trudging through snow. The annual cheer (a limited time, when young-adult friends commune and dive deep into the ravine of shared cherished times).

It ended.

★

My parent's faces.

I said goodbye.

I hit the road.

I was back to school for the New Year.

A day after returning to school, Vivian and I got a hotel-room and did the usual—back to love and blindness. Her parents went away in January, which left the house free for me to stay over and have it to ourselves. I slept there each night of the week. It was a glimpse of us living together in day-to-day adult life, with work, meals, leisure and rest.

One night, she curled her hair and put on lingerie so we could have passionate sex. But the episode of that staff party, three weeks prior, was far from a state of closure, so I hounded her for explanations and desperate apologies. Our fight began in the late afternoon and lasted until dawn of the next day. We laid apposed and silent on the bed sniffling in darkness.

I smashed my fist through the wall in front of me. A perfect hole.

"What the fuck, Rive? Oh my God, why would you do that?" she said, rolling over and seeing what I had done to her wall.

I started laughing.

"It's not funny. Are you serious?" she yelled.

I rolled on top of her, embracing her arms, sticking my face to hers, saying, "Ooooo, what's wrong, shmusems?" In a goo-goo-gaa-gaa voice (signature of our childish, carefree, impulsive and senseless love). Our infatuation with each other. We began kissing and she rolled onto me, so I laid on my back knowing she would give me head. She did and we made love.

But the fight carried over to the next night and it did not end with our flesh entwined. I had been snooping through messages on her laptop and found some with a guy from that party. He had invited her to another party. She replied: *Yes*— with exclamations and smiley-faces.

When she came up to the room I spared no time to give her hell. She tried to get the laptop from me, but I held it away and shoved back with my shoulder as I wandered around the house, screaming at her. She begged for me to give it back. I motioned to smash it, and she let out a wail not to do, as she had paid for the laptop with her own money.

We made our way to the kitchen, aimless and distraught. She took hold of the laptop, but I yanked back, pulling her to the ground. She wept as I marched back upstairs.

The battle continued in her room with our cries and hollers until I sat weeping on her bed. She screamed in horror and demanded me to leave. My begging and cries were reminiscent of those with Kailey: the same scamper, lost, following around a room. Vivian was terrified.

"Get out," she shrieked her loudest.

I stood outside her room sobbing out pathetic groans in beg and plea of her forgiveness and assurance that everything would be okay if I left. I asked her over and over, "Please don't call anyone, please Vivian," because she was threatened and pretended to be on the phone with her mom while I bawled on the floor. "Okay," I said, with a wobbling voice as I dragged my ass like a fussing toddler down each stair. "I'm going. Vivian, I'm going." But all she could say was, "Get out."

I whimpered. "I'm so sorry," I said, then staggered out the door.

I drove home to an unknown song from whatever album was playing in the car. I put down the window and lit a cigarette.

We talked the next day and hung-out within the week. By then her parents had returned and I fret of their discovery of the hole I put in her bedroom wall. When they did and asked her what happened she said she got mad one night and kicked the wall in anger not realizing the damage. They did not believe that.

Our time spent together became less frequent as the month went on. One day we went to a coffee shop to talk and I yelled at her with no consideration of those around watching appalled. With no escape from the rage she rushed to the bathroom and I sat in disgrace with my head down glancing at a woman who stared.

We left to my car as soon as she returned but I didn't stop arguing, while she cried in the passenger seat with no words. Soon tired out, I said no more and we had another countless make-up babble, snuggle and kiss. Then I dropped her off.

From that day on, and the following two weeks, she ignored me. I kept calling and sending massive messages of distress and need for her assurance that she still loved me and that we were still together. Then it was March and I received the response that I long waited in a desperate, feeble and maggoty curled-up carcass.

She told me that things had escalated, things were getting worse. She had told her friend, who hated me to the core, about the night of the party and nights I stayed over, which meant that she knew of my actions. Her brother knew also. He called me. He warned to stay away from her and to refrain from communication.

Something was wrong in a grave and severe course that would bring full the consequence for all that I had done. It was in the air. In her words. In my spirit. The moment before a coming catastrophe.

PART II

A Bony Sculpture

Here began the madness.

"Hey! You goin' to the big house?" said an unseen man. The voice seemed Latin-American and unconcerned about its situation.

"I don't know," I said.

On elevated concrete, called a bed, which was the exact length and width of an average man, sat a young one: as tall as one, underweight than most, privileged beyond many, and in a worse place than the average—not just young man—but North American citizen. So I thought.

The bed went wall to wall, its width halfway to the other, with a thin, more than used cushion on the concrete, called a mattress, where I sat looking forward.

"Hey! Some food, eh! Hey!" said the unseen. "You wanna sandwich man?—Hey! Give us sandwiches here."

I, the young man, grinned but was tormented. I had seen the Funny Man being walked to his cell further down the hall to the right and heard another in the cell to the left, but the Quiet Man must have been asleep. The funny man yelled again for sandwiches.

"Alright, Freddy, alright," said one of them. An officer's ratty steps heard to the left passed the bars, on to the right, silenced the Funny Man and ratted back, stopping at the bars offering me what was called a sandwich. "One or two."

"Just one." I said. I took a slice of boloney held by bread with light mustard. Forcing himself to eat, a slow chew and rushed swallow, while restricting my throat and mind by everything that was and is, because of who I was and had been, punishment was due. But the gag was in the fact that I had no set time or guarantee of its end—punishment. They would not give me a Bible. No windows to give light. No shoes—they took them. Baloney fucking sandwiches.

The world was cold and hard, suffocating hope, leaving no love. I once had love. It was the last thought to plunge my skull, from the fiery flood, before falling asleep for twelve minutes.

I awoke. The Funny Man must have fallen asleep. There were few noises. They told me earlier that I would be leaving bright and early for the courts. They told me few things, but those things and the things I told himself, were all there were to entertain.

★

I had arrived at nine the night before, after being arrested in the parking lot at school when I returned from soccer, which Vivian did not attend. A friend called me when I was getting changed after my game. He said the police were walking around campus looking for me, and I told him to let them know that I was on my way back to school. He was confused and questioned it all but said that it was fine. I knew what was happening.

I did. I knew someone made the call. When I got back from soccer they were waiting in the parking lot and I walked to them then was arrested wearing a t-shirt and shorts in the winter because I was sweating from the game, but that had cooled and faded so I shook in the back of the cop car, crammed without room for a budge. But the ride, congest and cuffs were not foreign as I made polite conversation with the officer in confidence and pride.

When I asked about life, where he went to school what program he took, I found out that he had attended Vivian's college when he was young. It was an odd coincidence. One of those odd random bits that pop up here and there in a life. Some give them no more attention than a shrug and puff from the nose, while others stroke their chin and mind in the clouds wading through possibilities and hidden meanings that could fit its shape (my father is without a doubt, a cloud-stroller—as am I. And my mother seems to be without a thought that random events could have a possible reason or purpose deeper than its brief time noticed and known), even if jammed by force, which I was doing as it was made to me a sign, omen, utterance and piece of the spiritual realm having entered my world and sense.

We arrived at the station and went through procedures, shoes taken away, standing, waiting, and letting. There was a man with a red tie and sharp face who looked like an ass.

After facing the wall waiting, and letting them feel my body for dangerous things, they took my shoes and put me in a tiny place with a phone so I could talk to duty counsel.

"Are you injured in any way? Have they treated you well?" asked a lady on the other end. She cared.

"No, I'm good."

"Okay, well they are going to ask you questions and you must not say a word, okay?"

"Alright."

"Nothing, don't tell them anything, just say that you have no comments and you do not wish to speak. They don't have the right to make you speak, and you have the right to remain silent, tell them you aren't saying a word."

"Okay, thank you," I said.

"No problem, and good luck." Such a sweet lady.

I knocked on the glass then they took me out and brought me into the detective's room. Sitting on a small circle, called a bench, I stared into the camera on the wall to piss them off. The detective entered, a woman, in her thirties.

"I'm sure you know that I'm not supposed to tell you anything, and that I should tell you that, so then what?" I said.

"Well, you don't have to say anything, but it will be helpful to talk about it, we need to hear your side of the story too, right?"

There was a lot to talk about, but it did not need to be talked about, because I took each word she spoke as lie. Nothing could help me except silence and time, but I was guilty and they already had the evidence, so there was no need for silence. There was no need for anything but time. Talking to the woman was better than sitting in a cell, it was fun, and passed the time. I asked for water. She came back and I told her everything.

Then she left, her voice could be heard from the room next door talking to a man. She talked the most and was the loudest. "I'm so smart." The woman was laughing. She was proud of her ability to get me to speak.

An officer came and grabbed me, taking me to my cell. Walked by two cells, one with a long-haired man, one empty, and then entered mine. There were a few more after and the Funny Man was in one of them. That's the gist of those past eight hours. I processed it all again, along with the things that were uncertain and unknown then fell asleep.

★

"Aright, get up."

It was time. Awaking when an officer came as I heard his steps and many other voices. I figured it was about 6:00 a.m. The officer opened the bars and brought me into a room with many things.

"Have a seat," said a woman.

A clock displayed 6:20 a.m. The woman took pictures from many angles. She placed my fingers and palms onto a screen which displayed all the lines and specifics, a digital canvass. She typed things into a computer and took pictures of my tattoos. Two, both religious: lyric on the inside and a verse on the outside of my forearm. She asked if they meant anything to me, a rhetorical question, and said that she hoped I'd learned from my choices. I said, "Yes," to everything. They brought me back to the cell and said I'd be leaving soon.

What I had done was wrong, and in most eyes, horrible. It could have been worse though. I was unlucky, that kind of thing happened all the time but many are not caught or have a phone call made to the police about their actions. I was caught. Though I had no idea if it was Vivian, her brother or what had led to my arrest. The thought of betrayal, a fist mushing my gut through its clenched fingers. I could not know if she was aware of what had happened to me, or if she tried to stop it.

"Alright, time to go," said an officer.

Finally. I was going to get out of there, but first the courts, and I had no idea what that meant or how close it was from being free. I thought of my mother's face.

An officer took me to a place, and gave back my shoes. They checked for dangerous things, cuffed my hands and feet with another man, the Long-Haired Man. We walked together into the back of a vehicle.

"Man, this is bull shit man," said the Long-Haired Man.

I liked the Long-Haired Man, he had years of smoking and drinking on his face. His hair was greasy and his voice was that of a late Bob Dylan. What a wonderful man. "Why are you here?" I asked.

"My old girl, she's fuckin' crazy man, bringing up shit from over a year ago, how I threw her phone at her. Fuck, I don't know."

"Yeah same. Sort of," I said.

"Woman man, but my lawyer will figure this shit out, she's fucked," he said.

I did not have a lawyer. Then the Funny Man was gone, and by the sound of it, wasn't going to the *big house*. And the Long-Haired Man didn't seem to have done much, had a lawyer, and was confident. Me, I had family. Good family that loved and supported me with money and things.

The vehicle stopped. Working together with the Long-Haired Man, chained, I shuffled out to the next place of what was expected to be a journey and experience one day to be looked back and mulled over. We were underground. The courts. Awful looking walls, and awful looking people were everywhere. It was not their faces, or their clothes, or their hair, or colors. They moved, defeated. If I was going to get out of there it was going to be after experiencing something. And things were going to become much more interesting, I knew.

The walls were white and numbered. Again, all the cells were on one side and they put me inside my own. It was much larger. A wall of glass and steel door with a slot for the working men and women, the officers, the city's law enforcement, government officials, keepers of the criminals for the decision makers to summon and sentence, to walk down the hall and look into all the cells, like held experiments through the glass in their three-walls of brick and shitter-also-water-fountain in the corner. Us creatures. Bad Ones. The ones who need correcting and re-education of proper conduct, social behavior and worldview for human civilization.

I walked to the metal shitter in my cell, pushed the button on top where the fountain was and drank. No beds, a concrete bench built into both walls. There were four cameras outside of the cell, on the wall and ceiling. There are odd and uncommon thoughts that come to a man who is held in a place like that, which was my hell of the moment. I thought of family and friends, the campus where I should have been safe in comfort and freedom, driving, drinking, holidays, cherished times and the life that seemed no longer mine but kidnapped and chained. Condemned for what was due for the deviance and decadence of my choices to take what I wanted without thought or care of family, friends, familiar or stranger.

"You want one?" There was an officer with sandwiches. He opened the slot and I slipped my hand to receive much needed food. Taking slow gnaws at the stale-dry bread with no desire for food being asked by the mind, but the gut a scavenging beggar. Orwell was right. Those cameras. At every turn of the eye I was watched and surveilled. One of them must have had a successful view of every damn move I could make, but there were four. Alright with me though, more chances of them to see my stare and dumb-ass grin with eyes pulled wide in foolishness and mockery. A bit of fun and attempt to piss off any who watched.

I feared not being free, for its obvious status but also prevention of me to attend work. Then I remembered that there was an assignment due in a few days as well. Stress and worry of the outside was strange as if mere memory or fabrication.

A lady tapped on the window.

"What's your name?" she asked.

I told her. She was from the Salvation Army, notching and scribbling on her clip-board as I answered her questions.

She asked if there was anyone that I wanted her to contact and make aware of my circumstance.

"Yes, my mother and my friend, Roy. He lives on campus at my school," I said.

"Ah yes, Servant Steps, I see. Interesting. And what is your mother's name?"

The use of my tongue to speak her name was a numb limb moving unknown.

"I will call her," she said then walked away. But she hesitated and came back, "Do you want a sweater? You look cold." Now there was a woman who represented the faith. I had been freezing since walking outside in the snow to the vehicle, then back out and placed eight floors under-ground without warmth to be offered from any dead brick-wall, miserable officer or imprisoned creature. Fetal in t-shirt and shorts.

Time passed.

"Rive?" An officer was at the door.

"Yeah."

"Going to see duty counsel." He motioned to be put my arms through the slot.

They were and then cuffed.

"Five," he said looking down the hall.

A blaring buzz, and the large door scraped open.

He brought me to a room attached with individual booths for prisoners to meet with their lawyers or counsel.

"Six," he said, "Press the buzzer when you're done."

At the sound, I entered the sixth chamber and saw another little stool-seat. Another glass wall, with a speaker built in but no one on the other side.

The cuffs were put on too tight. I leaned forward and put my forearms on my thighs, merging my hands, head down, eyes set to the door on the other side until it opened.

A woman sat down and began with my name, "Rive Devault."

I nodded.

"Okay. Rive your mother knows you are here but she has not arrived yet and your friend, Roy, is here. He does not have many assets so reaching an agreement for your bail is difficult. However, you live with him on residence at your school so that helps if he were to sign as surety. We are still in the process of figuring all this out."

"Alright," I said. She left and I pressed the buzzer.

I was put in a new cell with three other men. No one talked. One paced, two sat still in their wait to be freed or put back in jail. I laid down.

Hours seemed to have passed. The courts closed at four, it was two, said a man. Then more tapping at the window.

"Rive. Your sweater." The lady shoved it through the slot.

"Thank you. Has my mom said anything yet?" I asked.

"No. We left a message."

So I knew that my mother had yet to know. When she found out she would cry and moan. Her cry and moan, one like when I woke up to from a near-death alcohol poisoning evening in high school. (Ah, I just remembered something else from that night, before going unconscious. I made my way into an arena during public skating night, up the stairs somehow, went in the washroom and grasped the counter panting, looking into the mirror, purging my teeth through a gaping grin, before smashing it with my fist. It did not break. I punched it. Again, yelling, "Ahhh fuck. Eh. Eh." It was hilarious to me, I was so happy).

The sweater was dark-green, old and washed too many times. On the arm stitched in white it read: MARK 13. Another random in a life that left me a choice to shrug or search for its meaning. It could have been the name and athletic number of its previous owner or a sign from God. I made note to look up chapter thirteen in the book of Mark when I had access to a bible. But it was almost four and I still had not seen the judge. No agreement for bail. My mother knew nothing and it was her and her assets needed to make an agreement. And so came the first real thought of jail. Imminent. A sharp-cut thought. Though fearful and disheartening it promised adventure and thrill. But I was cold and hungry in hell.

One of the men had left to see someone and did not return. Then I saw the Long-Haired Man leave and never pass back by my cell. He had been freed too. And another left, leaving one other man in my cell. I laid back down watching him pace. Eight hours was the total time of imprisonment. There were fewer officers and criminals walking around.

Down the hall some ways were low-life young women, laughing in churls and boorish talk about nothing of meaning or value. Vulgar and simple critters. I hated that they could find humor in their bust and defeat.

"Let me out," wailed from the cell beside me.

This man's words could not be understood without hearing for oneself. A tall slow-man. I had seen him earlier. A big thick brute that had been walked to his cell with an officer on each side of him. Every word out of his mouth was wailed and slow like his being.

"Huuuyyy." Over and over again.

The officers ignored him. Other prisoners got pissed and told him to shut the fuck up.

"You shut the fuck up," he responded right back, much clearer than his grumbles. I listened to the exchange of curse and insult. A taste of soon coming jail, I thought.

At that point I reached the flustered and panic stage of my state. It was ridiculous. All that had led to it was unconceivable, absurd chaos that could have ended in many other ways than me behind the glass covered in cameras, peppered by drivel and libel. My thoughts drew close and dangerous to a feast of denying God: if he was present and existing I could blame him for my choices because all he could had to do was speak and warn me. He could have tampered with my free-will, choice, and behavior.

Regardless, I questioned and accused him for allowing me to make choices that led to damnation instead of wiping the thoughts from mind which gave rise my actions. One among many intriguing questions and dilemmas of Christian theology. God's govern over all while our souls live out in free-will and his sovereign-reign is kept intact. Never tweaking our wills (it is an endless debate whether God, being omnipotent, can manipulate human free-will through means of influence, hint or nudge, without taking away freedom of choice and decision or his interference and altering) yet he his hand enters our world to intervene when and how he pleases.

"Huuuhheyy." The Slow-Man was back at it.

Standing with my head on the glass I felt full-presence of the spirit which escorted my body through the holler, derision, degradation, and spite then, in the place where I stood. It rippled along my cold and bump-tight skin darting out words in its tongue of personal design, reiteration, repetition, identification, harassment and condemnation to be driven in my skull without free-will or chance to be rejected or refused. Sentences of my own and regular, but rooted in the form of thousands which were carved relentless from roof to floor on the walls of my mind far from any of the good works. Engraved by the tongues of my mother and father.

Nothing in my appearance was fearful or intimidating except the fidget of my hands, which displayed madness. Mad to handle, grip and tear apart order. Mad to the gnash of teeth in loathe and hatred of self. Held to a dwelling made fit for a soul worth the hand-full of change as mine.

"Let me out," screamed the Slow-Man.

I grunted breaths through the nose using the last of patience then screamed back, "Shut the fuck up." I slammed my first to the glass. The deliver and boom of my voice left no answer. It was my order given without expectance of refute or further thwart from the enemy. The voice that had made many cry, stop, and lose. No more sound. I knew that I would not be freed.

It was time.

Hands through and cuffed then buzzing, the lugging door, and an officer to take me somewhere.

We were put into a vehicle.

I was placed with the others. Most were older than me, thirties and forties. There was a guy who looked my age. His clothes were flashy, too famous, his hair was styled and grand, real fashionable, white-teethed and cocky. I got cuffed with this fancy man, hands and feet then shuffled into the back of a vehicle. It had three compartments for prisoners. One from the back and two form the side. The Slow-Man was put in alone, and the group of ninnies, naïve and proud, in the other.

The Fancy-Man and I sat in our metal chamber. I held my chin tight and eyes rugged.

"So, what did you do?" he asked.

"It doesn't matter."

He wasn't a threat. An affectionate chummy guy.

"This is brutal eh," I said relaxing my feet up against the wall in front of me.

"Yeah. Drinking and driving for me, yo!" said the Fancy-Man with a snicker a sneer.

His name was Rommel. Failing to show at his court date for drinking and driving got him arrested and here. But he was confident that he would be released the next day and it was evident in his smile and strut.

Rommel was a visionary. The post-modern type that tossed around daisies blabbering self-defeating and contradictive truth statements, "I'm a Christian, too. God is every-where man, there is no evil, no such thing. People need to focus on what's good and positive, there's no such thing as evil man, only good."

I frowned at his face and shook my head away bewildered. A what-the-fuck-are-you-talking-about without speaking. No evil he said. I wanted to ask if he had read even a passage of the Bible, a history book or ever watched the news. Life and truth in his mind were relative. I wanted to ask him if I could kill his mother and piss on her grace—give me a reason not to. It would not be evil because there is no such thing. But I held back my pride.

"Huuuhheyy."

The young women laughed at their crude jokes the entire way as if coming home drunk from a party. Then they shouted unknown things at the Slow-Man whenever he moaned. All of the voices could be heard.

We arrived. It was real. The walls were angry, floors burning and bodies being punished inside the prison of my enhanced hell. I believed in spiritual-warfare and this was a time that I felt it presented itself. A dangerous place. Not the drunk-tank anymore. The big-house where being killed is a real possible end to the stay.

I was not afraid. The thrill and adrenaline made me mindful and aware of each word, thought and surrounding. We, the new prisoners were put into lines to meet with officers and fill-out forms, get our pictures taken. I saw the nurse. I took no meds so there was not much to do or be said, but they gave me a needle to check for disease. Then I was handed my new outfit: orange-jumpsuit and slippers.

We stripped in front of the officers.

"Could I get some lotion for my tattoo? It's recent and I don't want it to get ruined." I said. I didn't know why I said it and realized the jest in its connotation. The officer watching laughed and taunted, but was confused as to whether the kid in front of him was serious.

"You are asking for lotion right now?" he said. "Just get dressed." Then he called out to tell an officer-pal the joke-of-the-day.

A mix of the new and regulars. An older prisoner, thirties I guessed, was in the stall beside me and frightening to look at. I watched the officer guarding his stall walk up to him and whisper in his ear, "Make sure you don't let us see it again alright? Hide it." It could have been a weapon, drugs or something that I could not think of. An example of the prison's inner-workings.

Dressed, I was sent with the others, both new and regular. We were assigned to different group holding-cells to eat dinner.

"Chicken or tuna?"

"Tuna," I said.

"Wow," said the officer, turning to another, "Hey. This guy asked for tuna." He turned back to me and said, "That's a first buddy." I was the object of their amusement twice within fifteen minutes of arrival. I sat with nine prisoners.

I did not know the routine, customs or norms, either said or understood by some criminal code. I began to eat from my plastic pre-made tray. An honest-to-god taste of shit, rank and spoil like burnt cat-food. Not much talking. Rommel was in a different cell.

"What does your tattoo say?" asked a man who was sat up leaning against the wall facing me the entire time, not eating. Looked to be thirty, buzzed head, comfortable, at home and confident in his experiences.

"Second Corinthians, four, sixteen to eighteen," I answered.

The man grinned and nodded. "And what verse is that?"

I forced a swallow of my cat-shit and squeaked out, "Therefore we do not lose heart. Though outwardly we are wasting away, yet inwardly we are being renewed day by day. For our light and momentary troubles are achieving for us an eternal glory that far outweighs them all. So we do not fix our eyes on what is seen, but on what is unseen, for what is seen is temporary, but what is unseen is eternal."

Another grin and nod.

"Alright let's go," yelled an officer.

Most prisoners were finished eating and began shuffling out. We formed another line and were put into our units waiting for our cell-number to be called. Rommel was in mine.

Being with him put me at ease because it was better than being with someone unknown and dangerous. Rommel was not dangerous just pompous and nerve-racking.

I was given four things: a cup, lethal-toothpaste, brush, and towel. We were sent to our cells and warned to make sure we shut the door behind us.

"I got top," said Rommel.

The cell was as expected. Small with a bunk bed and filthy and a metal toilet-fountain in the corner. There was something that impressed me though, cutouts of clocks from magazines so that the prisoners could tell the time. The work of some fugitive-genius. The rest of the cutouts were of half-naked women that were pasted throughout, most of them on the wall at the head of the bed for obvious reasons. Prisoners are smart.

There was garbage and grime scattered everywhere I stood, sat or laid. But there was a small desk and a pencil on top. Dull, but a pencil. I imaged me writing like those folk who'd been jailed and scribbled out magic from an inch-long piece of led.

"Do you think you'll get out tomorrow?" asked Rommel.

"I don't know. My parents live in Spinedune and still don't know that I've been arrested. I don't know how long for them to come and bail me out."

"You'll get out man. Tomorrow. We're getting out to-morrow. Both of us are getting out of here," he assured without reason.

I had come to appreciate his positive attitude because I was nauseous and afraid, trying to ready myself for adaptation of that world if I could not be freed the next day at the courts and had to come back. I gave all my energy to pointless, irrel-evant and unknown thoughts: would Roy come back again the next day, did my mother get the message, would she, or have me bailed before the courts closed. Did Vivian know what had happened? Did she understand what she had done? Did she do it? Did she know? She let it all happen.

"Let's get some sleep," said Rommel then shut-off the lights.

I laid down staring at the stains and things on the walls, trying not to move or think. The thoughts pulsed: I am in jail. I cannot get out. It could be days. I am in jail. Her. Vivian. Why have you forsaken me? Vivian. Friends. Roy. God. Help me.

I fell asleep in a hell.

★

A face jolted back from the window of our cell door.

The light flashed on and off. There were muffled voices shouting and impatient. "Rommel. Get up," I said getting up and looking out the door. It had to have been morning. We had slept in.

"Hurry the fuck up," snarled the voice.

My mouth was dry and I lapped for water in the few seconds I could while slipping on my shoes and preparing to be scolded, made to be unlearned, unaccustomed and a fool in front of the other criminals, or worse. "We have to go right now," I said, then left him behind.

"Let's fucking go," the voice kept on.

I joined the prisoners. It was the group to leave for the courts. A clock read: 6:00 a.m.

"You get up when we call you to get up, alright?" said an officer mad-as-hell shaking his fist in my face. "Boys won't be too happy with you two tonight when you get back," he threatened. It stirred my anger for the first time since being arrested. He could have opened our cell door and woken us, but instead he screamed to wake the regular prisons so he could blame it on us and have us beat. Piece of shit. All of the officers were cloddish and churlish men, troubled and oppressed by their shitty jobs looking after the dirt-shit humans of society.

Back to a group-cell for breakfast in brown paper-bag: stale bagel, package of jam and a bag of juice. We all hurried to eat, not just because we were hungry, but because there was little time before being ordered like slaves to go somewhere else.

After watching the others rip open the juice-bags with their teeth I followed suite. Slashing at gummy-jam to any form of a spread on my bread, fumbling around trying to do the most simple of tasks to able to eat, trying to appear casual and poised.

A man across from me with long hair on his head and face kept talking, sharing his thoughts, memories, ideas, tricks and swindles of the system. He seemed happy. Most ignored him and of the few that listened, not one gave full attention. Some looked like they wanted to strike him down. Routine. Another day. The Happy Man riffled through government news, conspiracies, ancient-civilizations, history and anything that he had been reading in the prison's library.

"What about you? You goin' to the courts this morning' pal?" said the Happy Man, like a friend to all with a smile struck on his bobbled-head.

"Yeah," I answered with mutual kindness.

"What'd you do?"

I told him my story.

Then he turned to Rommel. He asked of his life and deeds but Rommel replied tried-tough, "It doesn't matter," his tongue wiping the bottom-lip and lowered-jaw.

The Happy Man stopped moving back-and-forth and bobbling his head. He stared into Rommel's character with a look of danger, damage and know-how. I could then see why he was in jail despite him being a general man of welcome and regular talk. He told us what to expect and was confident that it would occur in the precise order and timing of which he stated. "So, there's a chance you boys get out today, but you might have to wait another day," he explained.

"No," snickered Rommel, "I'm getting out of here today."

The Happy Man tore his eyes into Rommel's face with a soft, mild and firm revision to the mark of his watch, which was the truth, nature, grit and volition of the pretty-boy ahead.

"No. You won't," said the Happy Man.

But Rommel scoffed and said, "Why?"

The Happy Man sat still. He smiled a crazed and loony-grin, then said, "Because that wouldn't be fair to any of us."

I wanted Rommel to shut-up because he had been associated with me and was a bad affiliate and presentation. So I kept talking to the Happy Man.

When I told him that I was about to graduate from bible college with a theology degree he poured information that I trusted as fact. He was well-read and intelligent. It felt good to have conversation and forget about the other prisoners around, some quiet and were most certain to be unsafe, uncaring, and unconcerned with consequence any longer.

Time was up. Officers brought us to another cell where the clothes that we wore on arrival hung in numbered bags from the ceiling. I found mine and dressed as fast that I could.

Then touched again. Felt, groped and searched for forbidden or dangerous things. Then cuffed and lined up. There was a man I had been keeping an eye on. Angry fellow the most I-have-been-in-prison-many-times look out of them all. Behind me in line, fist-clenched as he walked to stand beside me and be chained, postured up big and tall, grimaced and nose-lipped. All the shit I hated in a man's stride.

"It's going to be cold," I said, chummy, like the Happy Man.

But the Angry Man was shaking his head before I said a word and said, "Don't fucking talk to me. I ain't talkin' to no fuckin' PC's."

I froze. I knew that a PC stood for 'Protective Care', which was where the rapists, child-molesters and general bitches were kept so that they wouldn't get beaten or killed by the regulars. I had been mistaken for one of them, and so were the rest of the prisoners chained in a line with me.

The angry-man kept mumbling to himself and swaying back-and-forth to his tight fists.

"I ain't no fuckin' PC man. I'll fucking kill you," said a man a few men down the line from me, who heard the accusation. The two men traded blows with their words on verge of their fists, and I stood in the middle. But an officer ended it in seconds after telling the Angry Man that the group he was with, including me, were not of PC's.

The Angry Man gave a respectful apology to the man who threatened to kill him. "Sorry man, thought you were PC's, no way was I being chained up with a bunch of them." But he did not apologize or acknowledge me despite our wrists and ankles chained as one.

We shuffled outside. I had been wearing flip-flops when I was arrested. Now there was three inches of snow. An officer made his fun as we got in the back of the vehicle, this time with three more men in the metal compartment.

The man who retaliated, who threatened to kill the Angry Man, could have been in his forties and a mobster. He sat to my left, quiet, while the Angry Man and his assumed good pal had conversation to my right. "Oh yeah, there we go," said the Angry Man as he pulled our hands to the seat metal seat for warmth.

"Sorry again for that back there, eh? I didn't know," he said to the Mobster Man who just nodded with a grunt.

"Fuckin' McDonald's, right in front of the prison, man. What are they trying to do to us?" said Angry Man's pal. You could see out a small window if you kept wiping away the fog. We were on our way to the courts.

No one spoke for what seemed to be fifteen-minutes. And I watched the Angry Man lean back from the corner of my eye then nod, towards me, to his pal. I expected a beating because I looked timid and weak. So I sat up straight with my head held high.

"What did you do, huh?" the Angry Man asked me.

"Got in a fight," I said.

"Girlfriend?"

"No. Well, sort of."

"Boyfriend?" The Angry Man and his pal laughed.

"No."

"Ever been in prison before?"

"No."

"Yeah, you don't seem like one of us, or like you belong here."

"I don't," I said.

The Angry Man and his friend told me what to expect when I saw the judge, the exact thing as Happy Man had said, that I'd get out of there that day. A caring act. I was like a little brother among the older, tough and cool. I no longer feared them. They made jokes about women, money, crime, laborious-work, and the life in prison, for the rest of the drive. I laughed along.

"You'll get out of here bud. You will," said the Angry Man.

We arrived at the courts.

Familiar and foreseen. The touching, searching, cuffing and cell.

I was alone again. Pacing over what to expect and all that the prisoners had said, feeling seasoned and a veteran for being behind the same glass. I wanted my sandwich.

Rommel was in a cell somewhere to my left or right and I didn't care but had a strange sense of brotherly-protectiveness over him surface to relevance for the slightest moment until shaken away by my head.

I decided that a try for sleep was of the most logical and productive option. It must have been eight by then so nothing would happen for hours except the giving of sandwiches.

Thursday. Yes, it was Thursday. My assignment was due the next day but it was small so I could finish it on time I if got out that day. But that didn't matter. And Monday, I had to work Monday. No doubt I would be out by then. Yes, that day. I would get out that day.

Five fucking cameras.

I reamed back my face and danced for them like the Joker getting fucked in the ass.

★

And here began the wretchedness.

But a new freedom that owed its birth and life to it.

Sandwiches.

I had fallen asleep and that good ol' tap on the glass for some baloney, mustard and bread woke me right up.

"Thank you," I said. Holding it with both hands munching away. Fuck, what a great day, then I saw that my tattoos were pealing.

"Duty council," said an officer that came at my last bite.

I slipped my hands to be cuffed and taken out into a bit of what seemed to be a freedom. Walking around the building and seeing into different rooms. I sat hunched on the stool waiting for the door on the other side of the glass to open and reveal the mystery man or woman whose job it was to look after me.

It was an older man. He slapped down his folders and sat squinting down through his glasses then huffed, "This is the kind of behavior that gets people killed," He tilted down his head and gleamed up his eyes to see me, the scoundrel through the glass, then grunted when I came into focus. "It is unacceptable behavior. People like *you* are the problem. You cannot walk around thinking you are above the law. Do you understand me? Your ignorance got you in a place like this." He paused to look at his papers. "I am trying to come to agreement with the crown. The only asset your friend, Roy, has is his laptop. So I must wait for your mother."

"Okay," I said, "Does my mother know where I am?"

"Yes, she is on her way." He pushed the papers aside and took off his glasses, "Do you understand what you have done? Your behavior has put you in jail and you deserve to be. What if you have to back to the prison tonight? What is stopping a big guy with nothing to lose from seeing you as easy prey and sending you out in a body-bag?"

I kept my head nodding and then he left after getting out the last of his lesson and lecture.

I was brought to a new cell.

"Don't whistle," said the man imprisoned with me.

I didn't realize my song until he demanded its silence.

"Why?" I asked.

The man stopped pacing in shock of my ignorance, "Just don't." He was younger than most of the others, late twenties and of Southern American heritage.

"But why?"

He shook his head. "Alright, whatever. But you don't whistle in jail," he said, then continued to pace. After fifteen-minutes he said, "Listen. When you get back to the prison, if you don't get out today, mind your own business and lay-low. When you shower, go in and close the curtain then get undressed. If you make a phone call, hold your shirt up to face like this, because people will wipe some shit on the phone and it could be infected. Alright?"

A caring act. It was nice to know that there was someone looking out for me if I was not freed and had to return. I fell asleep confident.

I awoke daunted.

But it was an officer. "Rive, duty counsel."

I was brought down the hall but turned right instead of left then got in an elevator going up. That meant one thing.

The ground-level floor.

"You are going to see the judge," said the officer, holding my arm as he unlocked a door. Though stiff cuffed and not yet sentenced, I entered and saw my freedom in the form that would be seen again.

My mother's face.

She sat out in the benches beside Roy, Louis and Peter (a retired couple who have been close friends of my parent for years.

They have attended Spinedune Community Church with our family for years. Peter is a man of few words or sign of emotion, but gentle, kind and easy to talk to. Louis had her entire career as a teacher in my public-school but she never taught me. She has a high, squeaky voice and the lay of words and hands like a mother and grandmother. They have a genuine care for my well-being as if I were their grandson) and my pastor, Mark. A surprise and joy. The old grump from duty-council sat across from me.

I sat in a box at the side of the room. The judge began and the grump stated all that was in place which should secure my release. I tried not took at my mother because she looked back with her dark, mascara-mess eyes of worry, heartbreak, disappointment and smother, framed by her anxious-thinned cheeks.

My restrictions: a year of probation, no communication with Vivian or anyone associated with her, curfew to be in my residence after ten in the evening, unless with one of my sureties whom were my mother and Roy, but really just Roy because I was at school away from my mother.

I would have to wait a few months until being sentenced. Probation was obvious but it would not start until I had been sentenced

But it was over. I was free.

Once uncuffed, I walked out of the courts to meet with everyone in the hallway. Big hugs. Pastor Mark had driven Mother to the courts because she was too distraught to drive. Mother asked me many questions. We all waited for me to get my paper-work, and Mother urged to go in one of the offices to ask if she could pay my fine right away and get it done with.

When I got my paper-work, I sat while all of them fellowshipped at distance. I went over my reality: pages and pages of information about the case, dates, police-reports, interview transcriptions, and at the end—Vivian's testament. The answer to my questions.

She had abandoned me. Disowned me—saying that we had never been in a romantic-relationship, that I came to the party unasked and wouldn't leave, and that I got mad and pushed her. She wrote, in great detail, the truth of my actions but lied about who I was in her life. She renounced our love and my being—the fact that she would call me each day, speaking of our future, uttering the potential for a promising marriage. She loved me.

But she did not love me. There was no chance in hell for our love if she could have me casted to the sea, dumped onto the fucking ground, tossed in the wind, and doomed like a bug flying into a flame. I fucking hated her. I hated her, I demanded. She had to be erased from my mind.

Mother handed me a pamphlet before we all left. It was a weird time, place, and group of people in my life. An odd moment. There seemed to be so little to say or do. The pamphlet was for a partner-assault-response program. It was not a requirement by the courts, but duty-counsel said it would help my sentencing. I would have time to complete the course before my next court date.

With nothing left to say or do, I hugged everyone goodbye and left with Roy.

Sunlight.

Early Afternoon.

The rush of it all—concrete, road, buildings, traffic, sky, humanity, freedom—compelled the unmovable decision to remove Vivian from my life, and that gave me a reborn vision for life. With a giddy-bop in my step, which I hadn't felt in too long—but lathered in dread—all I could do was smile and lift my face to the heat, looking in the sun until my eyes burned. I threw my arms around Roy's tall-lank frame and yelled, "Eh-hhaaaahh my brother."

"Man, I'm so glad you're alright," he said.

I sensed that all the events and circumstances exited Roy because he had never experienced being in opposition to the law, whereas I'd had various encounters throughout high school: smoking-up and having fires on the beach, dining-and-dashing at the diner down town, getting wasted in the town arena for public skating nights (a major social event in high school), and stealing hockey jerseys from the local sports store. But this was different.

This was a ball and chain.

My life had been gutted. I was aching deep and below—in the depths of the truest void, in the darkest, thundering, and most violent storms of my soul. My spirit gagged on its flesh.

This was my arrival—to the inevitable trench of moaning tears and wailing regrets—from a chosen and carefree path.

For the first week of returning to school and society, I had a fear of everything and shook unlike my regular sooth-rocking—spooked and skittish. I spent most of my time in my room and stopped caring about my appearance and hygiene. I developed a stoic fasting of the eager drudge and social flash that I saw—too much and too often—in so many people, any place that I went.

★

(One month later)

"This is it," said a girl.

"Thank you," I said, nodding then turning towards the aisle.

I was probably walking fast. The thought was pulsing, unformed and unaddressed. It had to be done that night.

The girl, a lone worker, must love this shift: three people in the store, young couple giggling by the condoms, and a girl in desperate need for dog food at 1:40 a.m. The XL sweater I used to cloth my before leaving my apartment, accompanied with stained sweatpants and the ambition of a child on Easter morning, gave her a low profile. No music was playing. I listen for what's in establishments: convenient stores, coffee shops, mall shops, automobile service shops, restaurants, movie theatres, book stores, anything with a consumer environment. I don't know why, and I didn't feel like thinking about it right then. Where's the dog food?

"He looks like a fag," said the giggling man to his gal, an aisle over. It was difficult to hear his voice but I could make out those words, not the others.

I was frightened. Not frightened, but curious with intent driven by unreasonable fear. I wasn't walking. This was a familiar situation and I planned on handling it well. The difficulty was in knowing the truth; assuming I could hear, the words were either about me, or by strange coincidence, not: if they weren't about me then the coincidence existed within the words relevance to the context. I did not think either of them saw me earlier, but if they did, the man seemed smug and that would explain everything. I had been standing for almost three minutes, sifting through the possible explanations. In the past I always convinced myself it was coincidence, tonight I want to be sure. I decided to make myself visible.

"He looks like a weirdo." They were still laughing.

I was at the end of the aisle, stopped again. My concerns grew to anger. Down to my right was the dog food. I picked up the biggest and most healthy looking bag. *I need to get out of here*, I thought.

The laughs had almost silenced so, wanting to make myself visible, I walked out and in front of the other aisle to see.

"Whatever, he's cute," said the young girl. She was placing a magazine back on the shelf. The title read, SPECIAL PEOPLE, and a young male celebrity was on the cover.

I was already past them, a few aisles. It was another co-incidence, I felt foolish. My fear of drawing attention is what draws attention. There was no one at the checkout; the girl was doing paperwork at the other counter. I could hear the couple heading towards me, still talking. The worker put down her pen and hurried to check us out.

"Find everything alright?"

She grabbed the bag without making eye contact.

"Yeah," I said.

I stared at the couple without turning my head. They were younger than I thought. Although young, the boy was tall and thick. His too-tight shirt made him look even more self-satisfied. I turned my head to look at him directly with the crack of a smile made by barely pulling back my cheeks. His knit brows told me to *fuck off.*

"That's thirty-four sixty," said the girl.

She looked around my age and was pretty. Keeping my head down, I said, "Debit," and had my card ready at the machine.

"Ok," she said.

The couple was whispering, giggling, and the girl was clinging to his sides, swaying, tossing her head and hair around. It took a while, it seemed, for the card to go through, and I stared into the machine. I was excited to leave and begin writing, but anxious about the process. Being anxious because of getting dog food at this hour and hearing words that trigger my low self-esteem, were even more frustrating.

"Do you want your receipt?" said the pretty girl.

She had a smile that made me think she was in my head; it was kind and sincere.

"No thanks." I scooped up the bag and walked fast. Escaping an uncomfortable environment is odd and exhilarating. My other hand was in my pocket squeezing coins and I continued outside.

The rain had finally come. I smiled because I had been waiting for a storm or at least rain. This wasn't a storm though, it was light rain, but enough to make the walk to the bus a different kind of thought-provoking. Checking my phone, like many people, is often reflex and the more I thought about it the more I felt like a mindless fool. I let go. Many drops had touched me now and my pace was at its full. The bus stop was a five-minute walk. The streets were quiet by the slightest amount in comparison to other nights. That's why I like rain. My headphones were also in my pocket but reaching for those, although reflex, is purposeful and fulfilling. However, I decided to wait so that I wouldn't spoil the experience.

The stop was around the corner, just over a minute. I could see a figure, probably a man, waiting.

The first line. Pulsing. What will I write? What will I say? Why do I want to say it? I needed to get home to answer those questions. My grip was slipping, the bag was heavy, and so was the rain.

The man sniffed, gagged, and growled up snot from his throat, spitting on the street. I was twenty yards away but it was personal to my ear. By the time the expression of disgust washed from my face, we were standing together.

"Hey, you don't happen to got a cigarette on ya, eh?" asked great company.

I had one—my last. That thought was depressing already, but to give it away, well shit. My first intent when I got home was to have a drink, get started, have a smoke, then come back stronger.

"Yeah." I scraped around my pocket. "There you go."

"Thanks," said the man. He put it in his mouth, faced the ground to shield it, and pulling a lighter from his pocket, lit the tiny fix.

"No problem man." It was a sincere response.

The man had strong eyes. He exhaled. Our stare into each other lasted seconds.

Puddles being smashed by tires could be heard. The bus arrived. It looked like me and the man would be the only two on. The bus stopped and I walked towards the opening door as the man began walking in the direction in which the bus would continue. I put in my coins and sat three quarters of the way down, by the window, sidewalk side. My headphones were almost in place as the bus began driving by the man. He looked straight ahead. The rain was heavy.

There's a real feeling of importance that comes with listening to music in a moving vehicle, which must be why it's a scene in so many movies. Add the rain, and this is perfect. But it is dreadful and I have no concrete thoughts. Not only did I not know how I would go about my future poems, or what they would be about, but I did not know why I wanted to write them. I didn't know if there needed to be a reason. Everything and no one told me to do it.

"Shit!" I said.

The driver pressed the breaks, realizing my lack of attention. I grabbed the bag and ran to the front.

"Thanks. Yeah, right here is good." The door opened.

It had been a long time since I had walked in the night. Every noise seemed to have a purpose in the night. With rain, much of the walk is shadowed by its noise, and that is its purpose.

"Yep, bing, do la, meekafooo!" I blurted aloud for no reason. Well, except to add to the uncomfortable silencing rain and the shadow, which my eyes and mind would call: everything. I needed to drink.

I walked down the road of my apartment. There were street lights but the light was dark and I lurked my head around, anxious and afraid. Afraid of what? I liked to think that I would unleash if I were to be confronted by a mugger or some form of threat. But I did not want confrontation, and it was unlikely there would be any. Bur why was I ready? Ready with rage and joy, not passive acceptance. Was my manner and stride presenting an invitation for confrontation, or a fear of it? It was neither. It was an unsought desire to be involved in nonsense, and confidence in experience. I loved my hometown; it's safe and familiar. I've never experienced any trouble that I haven't provoked myself in my town.

But I wasn't in my town.

I was still in the city of my bible college.

I was beginning the first of two years at a seminary in Toronto for my Master's degree.

It was almost October. Fall had begun. Twice a week I took the train for a two hour ride to the big city. I would smoke a joint before boarding the train. Read, listen to music and stare out the window as I watched the trees become less and the concrete become more frequent. I watched the towers of Toronto get closer as the train pulled into the station and humans moved everywhere. I went underground and sat in the subway in the early morning where people were at the onslaught of their days. After the subway I took a bus which left me a fifteen-minute walk to the seminary. It was my new school. Not being on residence made it difficult to meet people, but I did not have that desire. Most people in my classes were older, established, professional men and women who were involved in ministry at local churches, social work, counselling, or education work settings.

Relationships with my peers were constrained to the hours I spent in class and during coffee breaks, those three days a week in Toronto. A few professors took a liking to me. One in particular, the World Religions and Philosophy professor, Dr. Jim Mavery, took time out of his schedule to have discussions of assignment, world affairs, theological concerns, and philosophical concepts. I appreciated these times.

After each day of classes, I would walk back to the bus stop, ride the subway for a half-hour, and board the train for the two hour ride. The difference being: the night, resuming its place in the world as I watched the towers of Toronto, lit up in their ways, pull away behind me outside the window. Business folk yapped on their phones about work, students stared at their phones or listened to music, many sat with their eyes closed, few read, and I kept my eyes, mind out the window. Watching the world pass. Change. I wanted to see it. Everything. I wanted to know it. But I felt that I knew—about all important truths, including that value of my soul— nothing.

School days went like that. The rest of the days I worked on assignments, drank, got high, and wrote poetry in the nearby café.

The weeks went by like that.

And there I was. Another night.

I walked the streets, high, needing, delusional and afraid.

The bag of dog food had been on my shoulder most of the way. My shoulder and arm were soar. I dropped it on the ground so I could get my key. There was no scratching at the door. I picked up the bag and went inside.

"Auden! What's up buddy?" I said.

Auden wasn't jumping up much. Something happened, he did something.

"Auden, what's wrong?" I was walking towards the kitchen. Something smelt awful, but it wasn't shit. I cut open the bag and filled his bowl.

"Alright boy, come here."

Auden did something. He stood head down, eyes up, and body turned away from me. His eyes were guilty. He definitely did something, and it has to do with the smell. I dove to the floor and tackled him.

"Come on! Come here! What's up?"

He relaxed in my arms and snuggled his head. I needed to write, but first I needed to find out what Auden did. There were only a few places to look. I walked into the kitchen.

There were many things: a bottle of whiskey, dishes, speaker, a plant, hotdog package, bouncy ball, and bread. There was nothing on the floor. I went into the living room.

Auden followed near and friendly, it was late and he was ready for bed. I picked up the papers scattered around the chair and put them together neatly on the table. The smell became stronger.

There was vomit in the corner, that's what Auden did.

"Man, no," I said, to both Auden and myself. Auden was shying away and I was walking towards the paper towels. My laptop was on the table by the papers. You have to write. I began scrubbing.

The vomit was almost cleaned up and Auden was out of sight. The laptop and papers have kept their existence known within my head, pulsing. I affirmed that I would finish cleaning this mess, have a drink, and write. There were no excuses, but there was fear. There is fear and it is dreadful.

I threw out the last of the paper towels and washed my hands. Auden's food was untouched. He isn't hungry since eating so much lately, and he doesn't want to go back to that kind of food.

"Auden."

He eventually came around the corner.

"It's all good buddy, you alright?" I sat on the floor holding my friend. I could see my laptop and papers in the other room. The fan was panning, and all the sounds of house and city masqueraded themselves as silence.

Write.

★

The abundance of my upbringing was the coat and finish on the glass-framed sculpture centered in the room of my mind.

But my mind had been trespassed, broken into, graffiti-riddled, window-bashed and at the mercy of its crook and pest that had no name, time of birth, family, friends, morals, goals or care. Smashed the glass-frame.

The flame of weld to the sculpture.

I never asked for money and things, not until they became expected, which developed to habit at an early age because my mother gave me most of what I wanted or asked for. I am guilty of rotting in greed. Yes, I know. I am aware. It is frustrating to be reminded, accused and called out for the repulsive, catered life given to me without choice.

But it is part of the meaning in the sculpture.

Of course, I didn't mind the money, comfort, toys, gifts, brand-news, having everything done for me and few desires left unfilled, but I made an effort to cut-loose from it. I told my mother that there was no need to buy me clothes because I had too many and didn't like the look or feel of that fashionable shit anyway. I told her to stop going in my room and cleaning, arranging and taking clothes to be put in the wash, which she did three to four times a week. Abnormal. It made no sense to me that people did laundry for clothes that were dirtied in no way except the idea of having been placed on the body for one day.

I told her not to make appointments for my hair to be cut, it wasn't long or unkept, and she was just high-handed, controlling and judgmental about appearance to the point of absolute disregard for other's soul and humanity. A seemingly superficial and depthless woman.

Her shelter, caress, routine, expectance, discomfort, and vain comforts drove me in search of all in opposition. I wanted pain, hail, discomfort, lack of resource and no way to know what came next. My thirst was for corruption, mystery, freedom, all that was raw, tainted, the company of outcasts and failures and a good time in harsh places to become a part of their survival and cycle. An edge where I stand to see the world and make decisions. The spoon of grit that stirs my anger and keeps it simmered fresh (my father has been of equal influence on the state, volume and management of temper, as well as my methods of handling undesirable situation, habitual strains of thought and impulsive behavioral responses, both he and my mother live out in me) to be indulged and savored at will.

I wanted to remove the assumption of my ignorance or compliance from people's thoughts. Because the course of the tracks and works on display are owed to my hand and its steadfast endeavor. A pledge to defiance, change and reversal of the pattern. The melding of the sculpture. The melding of all I was.

The melding of my soul.

By the hand of a Crook taking his time and the beauty. Mangling, distorting and recreating. Burning at the coat and finish, away of impressions and voices, allowing the new.

★

Now.

This is my current state:

I stroke the edges of my ribs in my bed, in the dark, where I hear and feel demons all over the room.

But we will get there. First, there is more.

I invented a future. I decided to go tree planting.

And that is what I think about as I curl up knee-to-chest into myself.

My bony sculpture.

PART III

The Bushes

I told you I would tell you about the demons who brought me to watch my mother choke.

Almost there.

I sold the dog.

Old Auden was my truest friend, but I could only afford his company for a few months. I had to sell him. I sold him to a cheery young gal who swore to take good care of him.

I moved back home to Spinedune.

I had finished the first year of my master's degree and was in the comfort of home to complete my second and final year. But there was no comfort.

The routine was the same. I drove Mother's car to the nearest train station, an hour away, took the train for two hours, sat in the subway for thirty-minutes, rode the bus for twenty, and walked fifteen, which brought me to the large, old, pious front door of my seminary in Toronto.

Being back at home was different: I was caged within the walls of a house that felt nothing like a home. During most evenings, I listened to Mother and Father tearing at each other's dignity with their words, ripping apart the seams of their marriage, and defeating the purpose of communication, vows, faith, and devotion.

I couldn't bear the dread of being in my home.

I spent the days drinking in my room, staying in that room, and leaving it to go to school, or outside, where I roamed my country road, got high, and smoked cigarettes. And then back to the room, where I would sit high, drinking, staring out the window at open fields and distant trees. When my parents went to bed, I would sneak outside in the middle of the night to get high again. Those times were different. There was a freedom in the night, outside in the wind with an open sky above. As the high reached my skull and stirred about warm thoughts and hopes, I savored a cigarette and knew that I was close to leaving.

Another Christmas passed.

A new year began and the cold died.

A friend of mine had planted trees up north for many summers. I asked him how to apply. I knew the money would be good, but I also knew it would be an adventure. I knew there would be open land, trees, and separation from the rat-race. I knew there would be interesting people, drinking, drugs, sex, and ecstasy.

So I went.

★

To the north.

It was May. I stood in Toronto surrounded by strangers my age. Most had planted before. I was a rookie and knew nothing and no one.

I waited for the bus alongside two guys, Jack and Ricky, who were also rookies. We got high.

We could see our breath now. It would get colder the further north.

The bus arrived. I sat in the back, pulled out my whiskey and sipped it, enjoying my high and everything out the window.

After six hours, we arrived in a small town of Northern Ontario.

We threw our bags in different vans that had met us there, and I stood around, silent and afraid of everyone around me. The people were unfamiliar and unknown. Before getting in one of the vans—sticking with Jack and Ricky—I kept my eyes on the different guys and girls: the girls for their potential beauty, and the boys for their potential companionship.

We made a stop for food and fuel.

I got out of the bus in the pissing rain and lugged my hockey bags full of gear to a trailer, and we drove out to the middle of no-where.

We drove for miles further north—through my favorite place—within the bushes, hills, and trees of the north. We coasted on a road, used, but not enough for pot-holes or faults, and nothing else around but forest and land. Our camp site came up alongside the road as a small dirt path that led to an open bowl of grass.

A field.

The grass was worn to the dirt. Hills surrounded and lead up, all around, to a deep and ample forest.

A sand path lead up to two ways. We went left. I followed everyone and did not know where to go. We pitched our tents, all of us rookies, and a few vets. I pitched my tent in the way that my one friend from home had told me was best. I did it as fast as I could. But it was just clustered and dumb. Then we had dinner.

And dinner was amazing. The lasagna, bread, salad, pasta—great. Your mother would stress and struggle to cook such a meal as cared and consistent that we had been served each and every day—to begin our journey. There was one woman—been doing it for years—and two assistants, who cooked for the camp.

Each morning we had a plentiful of beans, bacon, eggs, porridge, pancakes, waffles and grill-cheese sandwiches. Then there was the spread for lunch. We packed full for our day. There was each condiment you could want. There were fruits and vegetables, and the day's baked goods and treats. It was grand.

After each meal—we walked back up the hill to our bushes.

After setting up our tents, we got rope and tarps to make Tarp City: a triumphant shelter for us to live under when the snow and rain made its way.

There was a guy named Ty: his sister was a vet, but it was his first year. He was a good guy. He helped me set things up for the camp site and showed his acknowledgment of duties.

It was getting cold in the nights as the month went on.

We began to plant trees.

We rookies learned to navigate the terrain.

On day one, I planted one-hundred-fifty-seven trees, and I had to replant them all. I got perfect quality the second time. It was all about quality and quantity. Learn quality first, and then the speed: the money.

So, we ate well.

Each morning (5 a.m.), after washing our dishes off in the sinks by the main trailer, I'd run up to my tent, have a hoot of weed, a swig of whiskey, and live the longest life of a cigarette on my was down the hill—when the sun was rising: I watched my breath in the air as I stood in the circle of the morning meeting.

We planted trees in open land of earth, dirt, trees, ditches and bog.

I sat under the night within the trees.

I had been tree planting for weeks, and our nights off were wild. We roared up and out to the moon on those nights.

Work days were long: 5:45 a.m. until 6:30 p.m.—some days went longer if the block (area of land) needed to be finished. On those days, we would be back by eight o'clock. But we ate well—better food then I could make, and more than seconds.

Our camp was divided into crews. I rode in a van with my crew to the block each morning. I planted alongside those young men and woman, and they became close friends in short time. After work, I had limited hours to commune before bed, if I wanted a good sleep. During those hours, we sat on stumps under the tarps, smoking, drinking, playing cards, and listening to music around a table that we had made with sticks and rope.

★

There was a guy named Brett.

Bret was in my crew, and we sat in the back of the van every morning: everyone called him back-seat-Brett.

He was a special guy because he had an ardent smile, long-hair, snug chatter, and he didn't give a fuck about any-thing nonessential. But not in a rude way: he was a real caring guy and had a good heart and soul. He always listened, wanting to know more about the conversation that someone was pre-senting. I thought we had a lot. We got high each night in the bushes, around our table made of sticks and rope.

And there was a girl named Casey. She was beautiful but had a boyfriend, and she was always with him. She was stunning with long roping hair. I loved her, but I did not say a word or do a thing.

And it was her and her boyfriend who gave me ecstasy—for the first time in my life, some more good sweet drugs.

And I was giddy-boppin' this one night because I did what they called a "hippie-flip", which is ecstasy and magic-mushrooms at the same time. And I added a bottle of whiskey that stayed in my hand. So, I was utterly fucked.

After ziggin' along to nothing and no one, spewing words at people I had never spoken to, Brett called me over for a game. And we lost that game of Flip-Cup—never sunk one. So we had to do the naked-mile.

Without a glance at each other, slurring curses of agreement, we stripped naked and trotted throughout the camp. But I went the long way. With a bottle of whiskey in my hand, I scampered around the bowl of land surrounding our camp, up high for all to see. I came back around towards the crowd, scurrying down the sand dune, and tried to do a front-flip somersault: I landed with a slam on the crook of my neck and ribs, but everyone loved it.

I didn't spill a drop. I huffed my body to its feet and puffed my back to the crowd, cheering, "Fucking EHHHHH."

I plopped my ass and balls in the dirt, sand, and grass.

I howled, "FOR THE DEAD," because it was absurd and vacuous but made me laugh every time—and the breath of it rose up to God. He must have been hating his child, if He were indeed real and I His.

"Alright, now get your clothes on," someone said. The crowd turned back to their rave and the night carried on.

There was an all-seeing-eye fire pit that hosted the ring of us. Most nights off I sat shy without words, but that night I stomped around everyone as close to the fire as I could without burning. I jolted and shoved myself towards it as if to fall because this eighteen-year-old cutie with spunk told me, "Rive, people are just trying to chill, so sit down." And I couldn't rip my smile off.

Brett and I had were drunk, talking about traveling. We talked about hitchhiking to the east coast because neither of us had had been there before, and he had hitchhiked around the United States before. Writing and travelling would not escape my head. In the forest, armed with a whiskey bottle and cigarettes, I knew I would leave. I would leave and I would write.

"We're goin' out east," I said, lowering my voice, drooling my way to his log-chair by the fire, and leaning in his ear.

"We're goin' out east brother!" I exclaimed.

That night I lay in my tent tightened to the bone. I tried to move but it would not work, and I just wailed out in hilarity to the night. And I could hear a couple going at it in a tent some yards away—everything could be heard in the bushes. I laughed and howled out to the sky, screaming out for nothing: that I was fucked and having a good time doing it.

It took me fifteen-minutes to get out of my tent. I took an alleviating, reveling, and steaming piss on the dirt around my tent: in the north of my country where nobody knows or cares. I could hear the couple giggling and the girl say, "I never knew that Rive was such an animal."

And that was what I was—I am.

All that was in my head: I am an animal.

Me: a wanting, tarnished, fucked up little creature that was licking his teeth, wriggling his gums and bleeding. Yes bleeding. I could feel it—I thought. I sat on the earth outside of my tent—stroking my gums all around—in rain and wind. Everyone slept as I thought about how I would have to wake them, because my teeth seemed to have been grinded down since I was so high.

Like a little animal looking for food and meat, because I was so hungry, my burning stomach starved, thirsting, and shaking.

I got myself into my tent after twenty-minutes of sitting barefoot in dirt and spit, not smoking a cigarette in my mouth, too stuck in blackness of the trees and sky.

In my tent, I could not unzip my backpack to get a book out: with no true intention to read, because I couldn't tell if I was chewing up my mouth. I did get the book out, but I couldn't open it—it fell out of my hands beside my fruitless body. I felt my skin pulling back into itself like an animal needing to hunt. My teeth felt like they had to be bleeding, because I could not feel the regular length of them. They were rotting away—tearing, grinding and salivating for the race.

The game.

The hate.

The kill.

The dust.

That was all I was.

And so I felt, again, the sooth and slime of my spit around my teeth as I wiped away at them, trying to know what was happening. But I was just hallucinating.

On drugs in the bushes.

★

Insanity.

Many people in history have haunted their thoughts of what they deem good—what they deem right. This *they*—such a finger pointed, head-up word: but I must use it, as I do not suggest I am different. And here I say: a person's form of insanity is relative.

Insanity is relative to contemporary social prudence.

But societies are erratic.

And I believe in absolute truth.

Regardless, what is important now is insanity. What is important is what we call insanity.

Repetition: this may be a factor—as Einstein has famously said. However, the identity if this thing—insanity—has always fascinated me.

My mother always looked to those who shower irregularly, live day-to-day, worry not of the next, and listen to tunes with a drink in their hand, as careless fools. These people, she says, are not good, are not right—these people, she says, are bad.

I look at people, my mothers, and bend my neck left, hard to a rip. My mothers, the always: eat this, have this, want this, take this, do this, be this.

I love food. We must eat food. I am aware that there are things that must occur for survival. I am aware that we are blessed, and there are many who do not have a fraction of our necessities. But there is a profound emptiness in perfection. Or perhaps it is the emptiness that arrives when perfection does not. How often does perfection arrive? If you think it ever does, then you are insane. That is why I rather roam starved and fed on thought.

And what is perfection? Is that, too, relative?

My mothers—the vultures of In-Place—are the ones who baffle me.

These are the ones who make me crave an insanity that is true and pure. An insanity that can be defined by some as enlightenment. An insanity that makes all the mothers weep, because their child is dead to the culture's course, and forsaken by the trending praised.

★

One day, in my land (mapped out by my supervisor), I was on a hill looking out onto a giant untouched lake. I looked to the lake and took in the life that I was atlas a part of: an open, endless, triumphant world. No one was around me. It was open Canadian land. And then I heard rustling.

There was a wolf.

But it stood still, staring at me, and carried on as if I was not even good enough for food or the bother.

We drank that night, at the only bar in the nearest small town where we spent our nights off.

The town Legion. It was in the basement and was ac-tually a decent bar. It had two televisions and two pool tables. Brett and I had some good times playing pool and drinking countless pitchers of beer.

One night, the firefighters were in town, so it was the tree planters, firefighters, and the three regular old French locals in the legion. Brett was real drunk that night, and he stumbled over to me.

He said, "HEY," hovering by my ear, "let's go play them buddy. I don't like 'em. Nah! I don't like 'em at all!" That was the first time I had seen Brett real bonked out of his standard, subdued self.

And so, as the days went on, I grew restless, leaving my tent late in the nights to look up at the stars and ponder my departure. There were a few days when I worked beside Brett (our land was together), and I walked over to him through the hills, trenches and swap, to tell him that I wanted to leave. He told me that things would get better, we were only halfway in the season, just starting to learn and make money.

But I wanted to go home and write. I would have to work—as a freelance essay writer—but I wanted to do that too. Knowing I could write essays and learn, in my own room, private, and by my bed.

But I also wanted to leave for anywhere. To go east and wonder. It made no sense, because I had nothing that I would need, and only two hockey bags to carry, which were not bags for travelling. So I dragged through each day, dropped off in the land, always wanting to leave.

One day-off, in camp, Brett had some good ol' mushrooms.

We ate them and walked barefoot through the forest, toward the river. The mushrooms kicked in as we got deep within the tress, so it took a while to find our way since there were no trails and we were both barefoot and high-as-hell.

By the water, there was only one small patch of grass to sit or lie down on. People went there to swim and be in the sun. Some guys and I had went down a few times to fish.

But today, on this sun-lit afternoon, day-off, soaring on 'shrooms, Brett and I brought our books and journals—to bask in reality and creation.

The day was warm. The wind drove around the lake, caressing its surface and sculpting waves. We hopped in for a quick swim before the leeches wiggled to our legs.

Brett read as I wrote down our day and time together. There was a white bird hovering on the water that I thought was a dove, but Brett didn't think it could be.

I said, "In the Bible, a dove is a symbol for the Holy Spirit. When Jesus was baptized, it says that the Spirit of God hovered over him like a dove."

Brett and I had good talks about religion on that day, high on mushrooms by the water—we talked more of the faith. I could sense his doubt and mind set in disbelief, but it didn't bother me, because I was used to that. Still, I wanted to nudge him, more than the others, because he had a mind and heart different than the rest, seeming to value logic and truth.

That was my favorite day while planting. A cherished time. And then came the night.

★

It was night off in-camp.

More chaos, because no one and nothing was around. I hippie-flipped, again.

"RIVE!" slurred Casey.

I ran down the sand-hill in my trench coat and joined a crowd. She grabbed on to me and snuggled her face on my chest. I was zooming, and stayed still. For all of my interest in her, it was strange that I offered no reaction to her through word or action, despite her frequent flirt and attention on nights-off.

I did not drink as much whiskey, so the flip didn't fuck me into a state of drool. It was three in the morning and those who were awake sat around the fire, so I joined. But it felt uncomfortable and strange to be there without a blind urge to socialize. Not sober, but I had no confidence or dare. Instead, angst and fear flowed with the substance in my veins. I wanted to leave but then people would watch, and they would think that I was weak or boring for going to bed. It was a foolish concern, but regardless of its sham, it always and must occur when I walked away or went somewhere alone. Many times, I could hear voices and words that without a doubt concerned me, but that time, I received no attention and got away safe.

Alone and miserable in my tent, I listened to a couple fuck, again. I made no sound and felt no joy, but could move and function, so I found my notebook, listening to the fire-crew as the drunkest of them howled.

And I whiskey-jotted:

★

Any bitty mighty-godly, four-limbed fronting honky-haughty, and glitter-lashing lovelies, ebb to me please—ebb to my arms.

You, flowed-over rims, make way to my mouth.

There's too many streaks, strokes and raging flags. Too-tight-bows so ribbon-wound tight on my throat. All you shoulder-badged and banging us, with so many not-once-lived, dead-at-suggested standards, burying us in the ground. So many suits and gobbling-high-chins, our money in their pockets as we watch them shape the symbols that rule.

Torch it through.

But first, slit—no—slash into the bellies of all the Told-Colors: the souls of thought in life's spectrum—any of old and any of new. Crunch about, nibble for truth, and sip from those that gave up blood. Then ebb to my arms, so I can get to know them, because I am alone.

Veiled, artful powers, paint their life a spirit unseen but amid to feed on us.

They dine up high around the Everything-Table.

The Everything-Table: its legs sunken into the drooping star-stroked curtain-dome of dinging forks and knives.

The Colors dine.

They laugh and gorge above our heads.

Tink, tink, clink, clink: colored glasses seal the deal for your soul: That thing—not bitty thing—that oils your working fists, dyes your scenic-sketching eyes, molds your printing feet, and colors your only All.

Your only All.

Your one breath in time.

Will you keep it?

Beads of spirit and color—from their careening-careless drink—drip blessed into rain for us.

But above, they are veiled. As slouched full, Lavender (One of many; they are unending), slavers out, "What can you do for me?" And groping-eyed, lust-grinned, Scarlet, swallows nose-breathing, hissing soft, "Ah, those legs. O yes, on your knees. Mhh, I control."

The sky drizzles down on us in a field (any place) of us hundreds (any number), rousing around drink-held-limbs and our bicker-echoed-heads with thirst, tales and thought.

A droplet plops on, mingling down, spanning out veiled inside the life of a drink. Chatter, chatter, sipped; to the booming lunge-slugged tones probing our guts with a bounce. Then plops on and in another potent bead. Ladies dip foot-waved.

Ebb to me please. Spinning skirts giddy-hop to men's clapping hands swooning high. Plop, sip, taste, sip, savor, as all our bodies lift to feet-stomp the dust.

I sit under canvas elbow-to-knee and hand-hugged, tone-leaning forth, ebbing back listened to my plop-patting shelter, studied to the fog that crawls about it then leaps with grace. Tink, clink, tink, clink, as the table grows loud as they stand riot-mocking snug and stumbling proud. Fixing its lavish suit, Crimson: "Eehhrraauu, of course. Ppfftt, take more." Clink, clank, shatter, as jewel-word spewing, Ivory, says, "Ladies and Gentlemen, sit so I may teach you." Shatter, shatter, clank, as the legions commune, spilling drink, and the sky showers down at our heads, pounding in our drinks. And bitty-boy-so-shy now pissing in a flame, honky-haughty money-fuckers check their clothes and posture, glitter-lashing lovelies lick breasts while rattle-assed and hunched. Please, ebb to my arms. I know what the colors say to you, because they shine out your mouth, and I know you can speak a new stroke, but you keep drinking spirits and not being your soul. Your only All, will you keep it or do we have to torch it through. As I, tried and sober, sit in my fog, pulling in hard, the burn of a smoke, letting out fingers, heavy-waltzing coiled to the sky for me alone. Alone and lost, I say aloud to the sky, "Unveil." Out of my mouth I see, and in my eyes I hear, Gray.

Its head jolts stunned, curled alone and starved in darkness away from the table. It gets up and walks through disordered taunts and jabs, grabbing a glass from the meal. Gentle, firm-eyed, a finite-life ponders to be sure, then pours it down, saying, "No, you must keep it. Oil your fists, dye the scenes, mold many prints, and color your All."

The sky strikes down igniting the field. I stand dread-soaked beneath a blowing canvass, dazed, disgusted of gray; assured it to be lifeless, pleasure-void and bare like its feeble sight. Walking out into the rain as the field burns, I will torch it through, for here I beg and you all scamper. Ebb to me lovelies, please, I weep in the dirt. You, flowed-over rims, make your way to my mouth. Come back, please, and I will drink to see your all.

But flaring rich, beamed above, casting false colors and the table in veil, is a roaring-glorified Gray.

★

I could feel spirits all around me.

I fell asleep wanting to leave again. The scenario cycled in me like an endless jack-in-the-back. In the morning, I would wake-up before the rest and go straight to my supervisor, pack up my things, say certain good-byes, and leave.

And I did.

Telling my supervisor that my grandmother was sick (which she had been for a while), but I said she had just been diagnosed with cancer. I left after everyone left in the vans one morning.

It was 6 a.m. when I left. Before leaving I walked to Brett's tent as he smoked his morning cigarette.

"I'm leaving," I said. "But I still want to go east. Either way, if you want to come, let me know."

"Here," said Brett, "I'll give you my email." He wrote it on a ripped piece of cardboard from a case of beer.

I tucked it in my bag, gave him a hug, and walked away.

The drive to the nearest town for a bus was an hour away. My supervisor took me and we talked about philosophers, literature and religion.

(In the town where we spent our days off, there was a thrift-store ran out of an old women's house. Two floors, full of clothes, furniture, ornaments, books, games, movies and random things. For five dollars you got a black barrage bag to fill with anything you wanted. The first time I went there I got a trench coat because it was warm and looked crazy with my bandana. After that I only got books. There was not a large selection but some good ones. I found a copy from the sixties of Malcolm Lowry's, Under the Volcano).

★

Mother's face.

    Familiar.

    I read Lowry's work and sat in wonder.

    Later that summer, friends and I went to a festival, in nearby port-town, which occurs each year. The streets were blocked off for all to roam. There are horses, rides, food, games, concerts and endless tables selling local goods. So we all went to the boat yard to watch the fireworks. A friend's parents had a boat worth a fortune. We could never take it out but at least sit and drink on it along with the other boat owners bobbing along the dock.

    Being at home made no sense. I could feel the cold coming. The ending of summer. Mother's car had been in the shop for months so I had no freedom, no way to get away. So at night I would sneak out to the side of the house and get high, having my cigarette, jolting my head around not to get caught.

    From my backyard I could see the mist of the Falls in the distance. My yard spans wide and the sky always has stars. I would wait for my high and look at them. All I thought was going to race back inside and burst out amazing poems but they would never come. I would just sneak to the darkness rushing through tip-toe up the stairs.

    There were times when my mother would be sitting in the room by the kitchen, waiting. She had troubles sleeping but

I always cursed out loud thinking of her spying on my every move.

The time had come for me to leave. I had ordered the things needed for my trip: pack, strove, propane, dried-meals, tent, sleeping-bag and compass.

When it came in the mail I gathered it all and placed it together in the corner of my room. Waiting for the day.

The last night of us all together, friends and I went to Derek's house by the lake. It was a gorgeous night, black, cooling, full-moon and many stars. We decided to go to the beach and swim, and when we arrive I got drunk. Stripping down to the nude and running into water.

With the light from the nearby houses lining the lake, you could see the bottom like being in a bath. Drunk and high, I kept swimming out as far as I could, thinking of Sylvia Plath and her swimming out to her desired death. I wanted to be free. Looking to the hovered moon and close enough United States on the horizon. There were no clouds, in the darkness, but the adventure of a glowing moon.

"Rive, come back," said one friend. "Where are you? At least say something."

I had swam far. "EHHYYYAAAA," I called out.

As I swam back it was like leaving the trail of my trip, stepping away and coming back from the mystery road. But I knew that I would soon have it all, leaving to unknown and not coming back.

Mother's car had come back from the shop. Father wanted to sell it. So that night I took it out after having some beers with the boys. I drove to my grandfather's grave. He was cremated, so I was looking for the concrete statue that held his ashes.

I stood in the rain.

I screamed in the rain.

To Him—my supposed Heavenly Father.
"Fucking answer me," I wailed to the sky.
Nothing.

★

Here began the hunt.

I begged for the truth of our existence.

Here began the path to where I am now.

I had been in contact with Brett when he finished planting. We made plans to leave for the east at the beginning of August.

It was the beginning of August.

A week before we would venture. One night, Mother and Father sat at the dinner table with me, and we tried to consume dinner—apprehensive silence.

There were shards of grief, razor-edges bursting through the air, and it all could be sensed in the pulse of our chewing. Mother attempted to swallow a morsel of mashed potatoes and failed. She gasped and choked. She gagged and coughed, inhaling for the reach of a breath. To my sense, it was because of the nerves. She could sense the tension of her son wanting to leave and tear from the path. She knew that her husband would soon be divorced. She knew that her family was rotting apart.

There were demons. Slithering, plotting, whispering, gouging, and drooling—demons had brought me to watch my mother choke.

They had followed me.

Mother spat out mush. She wiped up her mess. Father shook his head and finished his meal. I went upstairs to my room.

That was the time my family would eat together at the table.

Many more grievous days passed. I remained bound to my room.

But time remained true. The day had come.

I was now leaving.

I had made an arrangement (online, with a retired man living in a large home) to rent in New Brunswick. After Brett and I were to make our way east and finish our trip, he was to fly home, and I was to stay.

My parents and grandmother were ready to take me to the train station and I would be on my way.

I hugged them goodbye and boarded the train. The same station that I had roamed for years when completing my master's degree.

On the train there was a family beside me from Scotland. I asked the father where they were heading, and he said, Toronto. I told him about my journey: I was trekking out east, embarking on a grand adventure, chasing down the fountain of life's holy nectar. The man just nodded, not giving a shit.

But I knew the meaning of my zeal, the power of my calling, the cost of my vicious charge to the gate of Hedonist Indulgence in Truth and End. I knew my path. To me, it was everything. To me, it was All. It was my hope to be free. It was my final righteous plea.

I was on my path to the peril-mystery of my Seek and Knock.

I arrived at a stop where Brett was to meet me. There was a thin fellah with a scraggly ponytail. He was an odd looking man, wandering on the phone. He walked over to me.

"It look like you are travelling some place, right?" he said.

"Yeah, I'm hitching out east with my pal," I said.

This man and I talked for a long time. He kept apologizing about his social skills and said that he does not often make an effort to talk to people. So for me, it was a cherished moment. I knew that our meeting and conversation was happening for a reason. I told him about my schooling and then we talked about religion, spirituality, and the things unknown.

"Man, I am glad I talked to you today, you know, this was actually great, I will remember this and keep this in my mind. You have opened my mind. This is what I needed," he said.

His family came to pick him up, and he went on his way.

So, I waited in the remote bus-stop.

Cars came and went. Another pulled in. I saw a woman driver and a longhaired passenger. Brett had arrived.

I swung my pack on and trotted forward, as Brett and his mother stepped out smiling.

"My brother," I said.

I opened my arms, threw back my head, and embraced Brett. I gave his mother a grand hug too.

"Oh, I'm a hunger!" I said. She blushed.

Brett's mother helped him unload his pack from the car. She gathered bags of snacks: trail mix, chocolate, dried fruit, and candy. She made sure her son had all that he needed.

After saying goodbye, Brett and I sat on the grass as he unpacked his bag, and we organized our things. Then began the ill of my gut. My nerves.

My consciousness of vexing angst, violent berating, and lauding sins.

I tried to eat his left-over pasta but could only swallow a few. We smoked some herb, had a cigarette, and swung up our packs to get on our way.

Under the sun, beginning my trip, afraid of everything.

We found a good spot on the side of the road, heading towards Ottawa. There wasn't much traffic, and the sun was edging beyond into holy expanse. So we sipped whiskey and talked of our time planting. Then came our first ride.

The first ride of our trip was a middle-aged woman.

"Listen boys." she said. "You have to behave because this is my first time picking up hitchhikers."

After jamming our shit into her car, we were on our way. She told us about her son: how he was our age and would have been doing the same kind of thing as us.

"Tree planting, that's what he did this summer for work," she said.

Brett and I looked at each other and laughed.

"Actually, that's how Rive and I met," said Brett. "We went planting this summer, met in the same camp, and decided to go out east." To me, it was an odd coincidence. But the woman just nodded and kept close to the wheel. The rest of the ride was quiet. I dozed off, and then we were on the side of the road again.

Our next ride was from an elderly man. With no hesitation to pick us up, pulling over right away. He told us about his times when he was our age, hitching throughout the world: Europe, Asia, Russia and South America.

He drove a simple car and was married with kids, but had one hell of a set of stories.

Our destination was Brett's cottage. We were close but needed one more ride. And we got it from three hipsters, our age, in a tiny car. A girl and two guys who were camping. Brett and I crammed in the back beside the one with dreads and a leather jacket. I had my pack on my lap, wrenching my neck and face against the window for the twenty minute ride. But we had made it to the road of Brett's cottage.

As they drove off, Brett said, "Now we smoke and drink, because we have a long hike." And then he said, "Fuck, I left my whiskey in their car."

Now dark. I got out my headlamp and we got high. And a van came by. So I flashed my light but they kept going. We were up north now and his cottage was back far in the bushes by the lake. Cars didn't come by often and it was late. But the van turned around.

It was a man with his family. A younger couple with their daughter and son.

"Where you boys heading?" asked the father.

"My dad has a cottage down here," said Brett.

"Well, let me drop my family off then I'll come back and get you."

So we walked up the road and waited for the man with his van. And he came back with his son and tossed in our gear. His son stared at us while he hopped in. I could feel his wonder, see the sparks in his mind of the little adventure that he and his father had embarked on. It was the same thoughts and hype that were mine as a child with my own father.

We were dropped off by the trail, and the man shook our hands wishing us luck. The boy waved goodbye as he and his father drove away.

Brett and I marched through the trees.

After the hike up the rocks, across the bridge, down the hill and around the shore, we arrived. His cottage was perfect. On the lake. Endless booze, good food.

Our first day, I slept in, waking to Brett sitting on the porch blowing smoke. We had some eggs, packed a lunch, got out the canoes, set-up our poles and journeyed the lake for the day. That was the time I had wanted. Barefoot, smoking, drinking, fishing for our dinner in the sun of the north, among trees, on rippling lakes. We paddled to the shore and carried our canoes to another lake, barefoot. There was something about that. As I stepped on rocks, scraped through sticks and trampled dirt. It was where Brett and I should be. I could see the joy and comfort from him. It was his place more than mine. Brett had made his journey and venture to that sort of life far before I had. He was raised in it. The definite choice and search for a life to be free. I saw him as the guide, couple years older than I, with those years having been fulfilled of the release. A release from the norm, expected, planned and regular. His journey in the States, the year prior, were his moments, that I was now seeking, by his side.

At night, we played crokinole (an Ontario game that you should look-into) and drank, getting high, having cigarettes under stars that outnumbered any breathes taken beneath them.

As we sat out and I looked to the sky, Brett laughed, saying how I will love his friend, Noah, because he too catches shooting stars at random and blurts it out.

"I'm always looking," I said.

"That's exactly what he says," Brett said.

Brett had made plans for us to go on a weeklong canoe trip in Quebec with his childhood friend, Noah, and Noah's friend, Jack.

Jack was said to be an experienced white-water paddler who spend weekends portaging random lakes in Ontario. I was excited to meet him.

After our week, we hiked through the woods, back on the road waiting for another gift of someone coming. And it only took a few minutes. Brett and I started with a great day. We began hiking from the cottage but there was a long road, six-kilometers, we are wishing to hitch a rare ride. We were heading to Ottawa.

Down the stone road towards a paved one, where small town folk drove sixty kilometers an hour through a speck on the map of my country, a truck drove down the road behind. As it slowed, I halted in the itch and joy that it would stop and be our next ride. It was. I knew our journey would keep going, and it would be a good day.

Frank—thank God for Frank. He happened to be coming by. Brett and I jumped in his truck. Frank took us toward the highway.

"Ever been to the east coast?" he asked. "Lots of nice people."

We stopped at the beer store. I guessed he was sixty-seven. A thin man, in decent shape. There was a bag of scotch-mints kept beside him in his truck.

He walked out of the store with a case of beer.

"On the road again," he said, as he flopped into the truck, grabbed another mint, slammed the door, lit a cigarette, inhaled, exhaled, and off we went.

Before our canoe trip we stopped in Northern Ontario to visit Brett's friend, Tim. He lived in the boonies, on a hill over-looking farms. A beautiful properly. At first it was difficult to eat when we began. At Tim's house, his friend, his gal and her friend prepared dinner. We sat around the table outside as they ate burgers, and I stared awkward near the sun, feeling the occasional eyes on me but more of the heat on my face—as they chewed, and I could only think of choking attempts to swallow. I wanted beer though.

Nothing special really happened that night. We tossed a football, got high, bopped around a hacky sack in the garage, and played a board game. I snuck cold pizza before bed. The next day we woke up and I only had a bit of popcorn before hitching to Ottawa. Before the ride I tried eating a sub but couldn't swallow without fear and hesitation.

So we were on our way to meet Noah outside of Ottawa. Tim dropped us off at a gas station. Brett and I walked down the road and met Noah at a Tim Hortons.

At first I thought he was a random, standing around. But it was Noah. He wore a weat-chewin-sun-hat above his long slim face, ratty and stained beige jeans loose to his thin frame, and a baggy plaid farm shirt. Our meeting was awkward. Our handshake naturally swung to an arm-wrestle grip as we pulled each other in with a pat on the back, semi-hugged. Our laughter made me know that we would get along.

"I'm a hugger," I told him.

We were heading to a river in northern Quebec.

And then we met up with Jack. An experienced paddler and serious. All the food, and plans for that matter, were prepared by him. He reminded me of my brother.

We headed up to Noah's worksite.

Noah had been working on the fringe of Quebec in a rural patch of land as a carpenter. He left home for the summer from Southern Ontario to live in the bushes and work two months steady. He brought a large tent to live in. He lived in it, thirty yards from the wood shop where he works, half-hour from Ottawa, in the trees of Quebec. It was a great set up. He had been living there in his tent for two months.

We sat out that night getting high, packing the seal-tight buoyant barrels with food and tools.

In the morning, we strapped the canoes to Jack's truck and left for the lake. I went with Jack, and Brett went with Noah. We stopped at a diner in the middle of nowhere.

As we soared down the hills past farm and field, sun rising, I looked to Jack with a smile, nodding my head.

"I've been listening to this guy," he said, raising the volume in his truck. And we lit cigarettes to guitar strapping tunes blaring out the window along with my arm battered by the wind.

"Oh we're goin' paddlin'," Jack hollered. And I eased back in the seat, rocking my head into echo strums, ONE, two, three, ONE, two, three, as the passing grass glistened with due.

After three hours of driving north, Noah went ahead to park his car at the end-point of the river. Jack and I picked Brett and Noah up, and we all went in the truck to the canoe launch at the beginning of the river and our journey.

Arriving by a bridge, we carried our gear and canoes down the gravel to the shore. We launched the canoes and were off on calm waters.

We eased through the wind and lining of tall trees. We paddled on.

All I saw were trees, to my left and right, blue sky—endless—and life-rich waters flowing ahead.

We parked our canoes on rocks of the shore.

We sat by the river. I wanted to get up to get my whiskey. I was always curious when Noah was talking.

In a moment, I could see Noah and Jack across the river weaving through trees, picking blueberries. It was blueberry season in Quebec so we gathered a bunch for our meals, or snagged a few to snack on when we walked to scope the rapids.

My mind craved mystery. I laid on a rock along the rapids, looking down the river opening into flat tree-mirrored water. Tall guiding green stood up to the bottom of white-dripped, all blue heavens.

Brett read distant behind me on the wide-spread flat rocks of the north that sloped into the rapids. I was reminded of our friendship, oh how faint and vague it was.

In the bushes we met, and in the bushes we were.

Most of our time had been spent in the middle of nowhere, far from regular things. The regular things: baths, soft material, full-fridge, television, movies, games, internet, social media, people.

I laid on that rock drinking whiskey away from the patch of dirt where we set up camp. I was in Quebec with a guy I had only spent a month in the bushes with, his friend, and that guy's friend. We had paddled for days, making good progress, now taking out our stoves to make dinner and enjoy it, secluded in the dirt, with no one around for ways. Only nature.

I thought of my further journey east.

The first set of rapids was a class-three. There are five classes, so three is for an experienced paddler. That is where we camped for the night. My gut stayed in my throat all day. Our first dinner we had steak and potatoes, and I remember from my first-aid training that steak was the most common food cause of choking. I had no appetite and told them that I didn't like steak, but it was fine because I wasn't hungry. But I took some potatoes and walked to the rocks with them.

I managed to swallow and eat, standing on the flat rocks by the rapids, as the sun was down and dusk took over. The water's rush and rapid's mist gave song. Then Noah came through the trees.

"Good one, eh?" he said, "We'll be runnin' it tomorrow." He smiled at the river in awe, nodding toward the rapid.

It was comforting that he came to see me and also that I had ate. We talked about the river, the rapids and our route through. Then we went back to get high with Brett and Jack.

In the morning, we had bacon and eggs. I had one slice and three mouthfuls. It was time to run my first rapid.

In the canoe, Brett and I pushed off and positioned, watching Jack and Noah go down first, and they did with ease. Our turn.

"Remember, yell for rocks, and steer us out of the way," said Brett.

We approached with soft paddling then the river took over. It sucked us through, and I held my paddle in the air doing nothing. No rocks yet. Then the first drop, entered straight, we slammed through waves and the water came in. Just as planned, we went through and well.

Noah and Jack cheered from downstream, raising their paddles. All smiles. I paddled shaking, doing nothing, and we joined up.

The second last day, as we paddled through the glass of the river, I saw a rainbow in the water and looked up just in time to announce it in the sky. We watched the last strip fade away.

"Aahhww yeah, fucking right! Rive saw that one. Wouldn't have seen if you weren't here Rive," said Noah.

So we spent our week smoking a plant of joy and sooth as we passed by the nature of creation, floating on the life source of life, sipping cigarettes, sucking maple hard-candy, breathing in the wind, and moving without the hint of a care for all the motion of a world that roared and tore in the universe.

It was over.

We pulled up our canoes at the end of the river.

Noah and Jack drove to get the truck, leaving Brett and I to wait.

Brett and I sat on am old wooden bridge reading and writing. A light breeze wiped some sun off my neck. I didn't move, just looked down the river. Fuck, I loved sitting in dirt, barefoot, flies landing to bite or try, far from busy, regular, expected and hurry. But I had an itch for Montreal. Soon, we would be there, and we would be in a bar drinking, shooting pool, with the French, or who knows?

After two hours, raging up dust, I saw Noah and Jack tearing down the gravel road. We loaded up and headed back to Noah's campsite.

We said goodbye to Jack.

Brett and I stayed the night at Noah's campsite. We pitched our tents. Before bed, we drank beer around a fire. Brett had a few, but Nate and I finished our six-packs. We talked about literature, childhood stories, old friends and memories.

The next day Nate drove us to the bus station.

★

Brett and I laid on cigarette-brick, against the wall of a Montreal mall.

We found a very cheap hostel and after wandering the city to find a good bar, we ended up back at the one underneath it. Convenient.

Brett swayed almost down and out the window. He was sitting on the ledge getting high.

It was 8:25 p.m., and I let Brett wander the city on his own. I should have went, but I was too lazy. My head hurt. I wasn't hungry, but I felt the nothing in my stomach and its need to be filled. I ate a piece of chicken that we picked up hours before, and it tasted like stale morning mouth.

I opened the windows. I sat on the ledge. An opening and entry to the city. I didn't like Montreal, but I hadn't seen much. Too lazy to care.

Brett returned and we wandered the streets. We wandered into Gay Village, without knowing. I thought I saw a pool table in a bar, so we entered. Full of seated folk watching some sort of show, a spot-lit person carried a microphone. The person wore a dress, with giant fake tits, a wig, makeup, jewelry, etc.

"Well look at these two cuties coming in." said the person.

"Bonjour," I replied with confidence.

"HA, bon-JOUR."

Everyone laughed, and the person squealed, all sass, saying, "Just have a seat, shut the fuck up, and have a good time."

We left. It took me a bit to realize that it was not a woman but indeed a man. I clenched my fist. So there we were, back at the hostel, in the basement pub. An under-ground feel, many tatted space-eared, city hip folk.

There were no stars. There were no clouds but no stars. Just the darkest blue glowing by the brick boxes with all us things moving around wanting, trying and fulfilling.

And so we sat in the basement pub with the city rats, tattooed hipsters and carousing French. After drinking two of three pitchers, I said, "That fucking guy, wish I knew it was, could've went at him."

"Those drag-queens would've kicked the shit out of you," said Brett, laughing.

And we argued as drunken pals in pride, releasing stored-up grievances. But it was a show of true friendship.

A guy with long hair and a little mustache, covered in tattoos, came over along with some girl in a black polo, also tattooed, but shaved head. In her thick accent, the girl asked if we wanted to play foosball: losers would buy shots. So we played and we won.

The next day and our last in Montreal, we walked downtown and saw famous sculptures, buildings and sights. Then we walked to the bus-stop.

There was a bookstore across the road and we had a half-hour wait for the bus so we went to look around. I had wanted a book for the trip. It was an older Chapter's from the outside, but updated inside and brand-new. So I didn't understand why there were zero works by Henry Miller. After looking through Bukowski, Kerouac and Tolstoy, I grabbed a copy of A Clockwork Orange by Anthony Burgess, then we got on the subway, took a bus away from the city, and found our place on roadside.

Before leaving the hostel I had couch-surfed online for a host in Quebec City. A guy named Michael responded and accepted within the hour so we were set. Then I scrolled through his profile and noticed the groups he joined: Gays of Toronto, Queers in Quebec, The Naked Party, Chicago's Queers, Gay Travelers in Vancouver, and the list went on.

"Brett, I think this guy might be gay," I said, handing him my phone. He read and laughed. "This will be good," he said.

We got high and tossed stones on the road at the on-ramp. A game to see who could get closest to the target which was a larger rock. It took three hours, but a guy gave us a ride in a work van with rotating cameras on top. In his late twenties, he worked for a mapping company photographing roads and locations. So the back was filled to the roof with hardware and software, leaving the one bench behind the driver where Brett and I sat. A desk with a laptop and folders took the place of a passenger seat.

This ride, Brett fell asleep and I stayed awake. The guy played his songs loud, and they were all familiar. One of them was from an old Christian rock-band that I had always listened to in high school.

"What you guys do in the city?" he asked.

"We're making our way to the coast, stopping in cities on the way, just touring around, going to bars and having a time," I said.

"You see building there? That is where you go if you want to have fun," he laughed, pointing to the city at distance, uphill on our path.

He dropped us off at a gas station on the base of the hill.

"I'm down for more hotdogs," I said, hoping each station we stopped at had them, and most did.

We ate in the grass. Got high on the curb. Then swung up our bags and went for the hill. It was a bitch.

Michael's apartment building was nice as expected.

We were in Quebec City.

Buzzing Michael's name.

Michael skipped to us.

"Oh hello, yes hello, yes okay!" he said, fussing while letting us in the building. "So! You must give me ten minutes, because I must clean up."

His apartment was the first one inside. Brett and I sat on the two waiting chairs which looked to have never been used, laughing while we listened to Daniel *oouughing* and *aahhwwing* as he swept his apartment. He would shriek in a high pitch, prancing feet, gleeful face and flapping arms. This became his signature way and presence in the thoughts of Brett and I throughout the rest our trip.

Once finished cleaning and ready for us, Michael gave joy and a warm welcome. His clothes: white and blue loose-fitted V-neck and cargo shorts. Nothing bright or fancy. Bit of a beard, short hair and lots on his chest. An average masculine man if not for his movements and speech. But one of the nicest people I'd ever met.

"AHHOO, look at your feet," he said. "Come here. Yes, yes, to the tub. You must wash them."

Brett and I looked at our feet. Our feet were black. Both of us wore flip-flops. So we washed our feet together in the tub, smiling at each other as Michael scurried about in the kitchen and spoke of his excitement for our visit.

The Olympics were on and Michael was obsessed with them. He shrieked and squealed at every move. "My T.V," he said wide-eyed, chin bent in sass, "is my life." He giggled and flung his finger side-to-side.

Our first night, Brett and I found a bar down the street near downtown. A small room, but it had a pool table and a good crowd. The bartender got us playing a game with coins. The rules: After each player flips, the minority is safe. So if four people flip three heads and one tails, the player who flipped tails is safe and out of the game, and this continues until two players remain. When the last two flip, one of them calls whether both coins will be the same or different. The last player remaining buys a round of drinks for every player. A great game, because the odds to be safe increase with more players, but whoever loses has a shit ton of drinks to buy.

Brett and I played five rounds with the tender and another guy we met. Each of us lost once, Brett twice. So we left dickered.

There was one bedroom in Michael's apartment, and it was where his roommate slept. Michael slept on a mattress in the living room, three-feet from the T.V. Brett and I slept on an air-mattress beside him. In the morning, waiting for them to awake, I watched Michael on each of his toes, stretching up both arms, slide hands down his face then neck and snap ahead with the wrists, flailing out to his sides. Then Brett awoke.

Michael pranced and bumbled about in only his high-socks and boxer-briefs. "Goocheeegooo!" he said, while tickling Brett's foot, as he passed by us on his toes.

Brett and I spent the day wandering downtown Old Quebec then went to a park and laid on the grass with our books and cigarettes. A family tossed a Frisbee, one couple sat talking and another walked dogs. There was a tall brick wall surrounding the park's central statue and a guy scaled it side-to-side, appearing to be an experienced climber. His girlfriend lay away on her chest facing towards him with an open book, but stayed watching him.

I had made it three-quarters through my book but fell asleep beside Brett who had been passed out for hours. When we awoke, the sun had just passed behind the trees as the grass and air cooled while making our way back to Michael's. He was watching the Olympics and cheered at our arrival. So we sat together for three hours watching and sipping the cinnamon-whiskey that we had bought Michael for letting us stay, which lit his eyes and spread open his mouth as he speed-clapped and praised us in joy and appreciation.

That night, Brett and I went to the same bar as the previous, but then further down the street to find another. No other place had a pool table, but one had crowds stumbling out-front, so we joined. An old wooden staircase narrowing high led up to the bar. It was full. Some sat, many danced, and few stood. After having a few we walked over to the foosball table where four folks our age played. One pretty gal and three guys. After being acquainted and getting to know one another, we played doubles. Brett and I faced one of the guys and the lovely, right in front me, controlling the bars on defense, as I was on offense. Each time I scored, we looked up and smiled.

But one of the guys—the nicest—was her boyfriend. Tall, pudgy, baby-faced, glasses and well-dressed. Of the other two guys, one was standoffish and proud at first, drunk, but palled around once he realized Brett and I weren't a threat and gave good company. The other guy was a bit different than them all: long-haired, jean-jacket, tattoos and a novel in hand as he read beside us on a stool. His name was Philippe-Dennis Dechaume. An intelligent young man. We talked of literature, spirituality, politics and Quebec's history.

As the bar closed, all shuffled out and down the street to a bar that stayed open another two hours. Now drunk, we sat at a table immersed in our talk. Brett, the gal and her man stayed to their own while the other two guys and myself discussed Quebec. I was real bonked and knew that out conversation wounded in a circle. Both kept mentioning the unfairness of Quebecers having to learn English while outsiders don't care to learn French and came into Quebec expecting to be heard and spoken to in English. I understood their point but told them that there are people who try and learn French and respect Quebec's culture. And the fact that many Canadian's first language is English has nothing to do with ignorance or spite, but demographics and geography. It's simply because most are born to English speaking parents in an English speaking area. If those two guys were born in my hometown to English parents then they would be one of whom they denounce. And if I had been born in Quebec, like some of my cousins, then I would be one of them.

But they just wanted to use their time with us outsiders to get out their displeasure and pride. And all I had to do was nod and be sorry, but I raised my voice and slammed my glass instead. So when we left, amidst drunken stumble, I didn't say goodbye or remember them leave my sight. Then Brett and I staggered down the road.

We argued the entire way. Michael's apartment was by the road a foot away from the sideway. He had told us to knock on the sliding-door when we were back. But we sat by on the concrete and got high as our debate heightened with our voices.

"Do you even know what they are talking about," said Brett. "They were telling me everything and I'm starting to feel like a separatist myself."

"I know, my family is from Quebec."

"Stop saying that, you sound like a little cunt," said Brett. "You don't even know the history, you know nothing about Quebec."

"I don't know much but those people were just trying to feel special, they like being different, and make no sense talking about being lesser when they choose to separate, as if those outside are the lesser, it's not black and white, us or them, it's too complicated and long-aged for anyone to be so set in their views," I said.

"Wow, you know what, I thought you were an open person, but you're close-minded."

It was back-and-forth until Michael tip-toped to the sliding door in his undies, whispering through the screen, "Guys, please, I can hear you. Yes, can you come in now?"

The next day and our last, we slept in, watched the Olympics come to an end, planned our next route and spoke nothing of the night before. After saying goodbye to Michael and bussing to the center of Quebec City, Brett and I toured along its old brick streets then took the ferry across the St. Lawrence River.

★

On the other side before us was a hell of a hike up a hill through small town streets. It took three hours to reach the highway. My calves torn, stomach bubbling acid and bones rubbing against the pack that doubled me in size.

Our ride was a heavy woman, early-thirties, long nails, half-shaven purple hair and hard on the gas. She wore large shades and drove with one-handed. Her backseat was messed with children's books, cracker crumbs, toys, cups and garbage. She told us about her five-year-old daughter, how cute and much of a monster she was. I imaged her to be a young punk like her mother.

"I take you to better place for hitchhiking, not far but at least you get a ride," she said. "You guys smoke weed?"

"Yeah, I'm surprised actually, we haven't met people that smoke," said Brett.

The woman laughed and invited us to her home.

She was not from Quebec, though spoke and sounded as if born there, moved and lived there for years. Her house was on the way to where she would drop us. Rural land. Her house was small but pleasurable, clean and organized. And he daughter was angel. She was shy and well-mannered. It could see that the woman was not immature like I assumed, she was a good mother and took good care of her child, providing, not spoiling, and teaching proper behavior.

"Abella, this is Brett and Rive. Say hello." But the little girl looked up a little smile and hands held fiddled, curious, and gentle, twisting playful.

We had a glass of water and went out on the deck. Abella ran free. The backyard was small and fenced in the same as each other one along both sides. But the neighborhood and homes were on a hill and provided a view of the open land afar running out to distant trees. Gorgeous on that day with sun, sweet herb and fun company.

"Come over here, Abella," said the woman, in a sweetened voice. And then back normal. "She doesn't like to speak English for some reason, but she can."

"I wish I knew French," I said.

"Why? You guys don't need French, but I need English." So we talked about Quebec, its language and people.

"Quebec sucks, screw it," she said, "I don't like Quebec."

"Really? Why?" said Brett.

"Because, people here are close-minded. You know? They are proud and think they are better."

Brett inhaled, shrugged and looked down. An odd coincidence in her choice of words. Brett and I never brought it up, but I gained a new understanding and respect from Brett for the rest of our travels.

After playing outside with Abella, the woman dropped us as a remote on-ramp. Ten-minutes later, I realized that my book was in her backseat.

"We should make a list of things we've lost," said Brett.

I took out my notepad: *Shit we've lost. My pen/Brett's whiskey and its bottle/My wallet (at Brett's cottage, but found)/ My phone (left in QBC bar, returned next day by random guy)/ Brett's spork/My book/Brett's phone/My pencil.*

Dusk came, then the night and streetlights above us. There was a radio tower nearby.

"If we have to campout tonight, we should get drunk and climb that," I said. We laughed planning our approach, how far up we'd go, whether we'd fall, and if we'd get caught.

Then came our ride. A thirty-year-old Middle-Eastern man in a beater. He had lived in Canada for most of his life, loved to travel, hike and help others. He drove us to Mont-magny.

It was early afternoon when we arrived and we waited until nine before going in the bushes right where we stood, because there was a clearing inside. We set up our tents, got out our stoves and whiskey, and cooked dinner.

Eight o'clock the next morning we packed up, wade through the bushes, and stood at our spot by the road.

A teacher named Nick picked us up, taking us to Saint-Jean Port-Joli. He was on his way to the first day of school, where he taught agriculture to college students. Along the way he told of his family and stories with them sailing the St. Lawrence, which ran with us along the way, as our heads kept left to marvel the mountains and open water's morning-sparkled waves. Nick sailed and biked often, keeping him fit, a handsome man. There was a hockey stick in the backseat, and I pictured in my mind his post-card children as he drove them to practice. And his wife, beautiful with class, greeting him home as she chopped potatoes and veggies for their every-day home-cooked meal. He was the man that I wished to be, but could never.

After Nick's kind wishes goodbye, Brett and I stood at the on-ramp of a highway much busier than what we had travelled. In less than an hour, our ride was a young, female-looking guy, taking us to Riviere-du-Loup.

He was shy but listened to damn good tunes. There was a skateboard in his backseat and headphones. A musician, he told us, drummer and singer. So I asked of his favorite artists, then we traded bands and none of us talked much after that. A good rest though, soothing, and time to think. He dropped us off, an hour walk from where we needed to be.

So we swung up our packs and walked the roads to our on-ramp. Lighting a pipe, I was refreshed with the thought that our next stop should be New Brunswick. And after two hours, our ride was an old and odd man. Hesitant and speaking minimal English but, "Come, come!" he said.

The back of his van had endless boxes filled with files. He was working, travelling for his company, and that's what he mumbled about when first pulling over, before realizing we gave no shits of his work or employer, with no chance of ratting him out, so he gave us a ride. After our names, no one spoke for the half-hour. But again, got dropped an hour away from where we needed to be. A nice guy though, smiled a lot.

And we entered New Brunswick.

So we swung up our packs and dragged ourselves down road-sides to Edmundston. After four hours, we got booze and found a great spot to camp behind a power station, on the road but sheltered with trees. No one could see us but we were close and saw everything. There was perfect grass for our tents.

That night, we drank all our whiskey and beer, got high and kissed cigarettes under stars far outnumbering our nights since our last on the water with Paddlin' Jack and Yip-Hootin' Noah.

We ran around barefoot, talking of things unseen. Most of the talks were of literature, philosophy, religion, politics, science and space. It was our best and happiest night together.

"It is interesting though, I never thought of the bible that way," he said.

"Well it's like any other document of history, which can be studied and verified. I like to look at the bible without all its flak, connotation and golden pages, but on plain white paper printed out alongside all the other ancient texts. Of any other ancient text, the Old and New Testament is by far, the most well sourced, reliable and historically accurate documents we have. Scholars have gathered enough evidence for Christ and his life using only sources outside of the bible, from ancient historians, scribes and writers. There are many prolific historians, both atheist and agnostic, who claim that the existence, death and crucifixion of Jesus Christ is historical fact. The question is, did he rise from the grave, because without that, there is no faith. And when looking at the accounts and their legitimacy, it seems to logical to believe that he did indeed rise again, as many claimed to see."

"But how do you know it wasn't just all made up, just a story for attention and control over people? Like look how the Catholic Church can be corrupted and control lives in fear." Brett said.

"But it's not that simple. The organized church didn't start until years after Jesus' life. You have to think of the immediate reality. His followers, and the hundreds who claimed to witness his resurrection, had nothing to gain and no way of controlling some made up story. The locals, never mind the Romans, would have squashed such a story if it were false, but instead, the largest movement in human history spread rapid because so many saw and believed. And think, why would they spread the gospel and write it all down if all for a lie that gained them no wealth, power or pleasure, but rather, it brought each one of them persecution, torture and death. No man would go so far for a lie that could simply be denounced. All I know, is that these people were dead-certain of what saw. And along with the historical, archeological and documental study, the words and teachings of Jesus are profound to say the least, having truth like no other."

I knew that I would not sway Brett from his views, but neither was it my intention. As I told him, I too was just another human at war with the truth of existence and reality. But I had reason for my beliefs, despite needing faith at the end of the day, as do we all. So after that topic, we discussed our lives and futures. Brett would be going back to Toronto at the end of the month for work in landscaping, and I was to stay east, renting and writing my first book of poetry.

"I just wish I could sit and rip through it," I said.

"You will man, honestly, you're going to get out there, on your own and inspired, then pound out your book, don't hold anything back, fuck what people will think or say, just write it all."

I loved drunk Brett encouraging me. As I said, our best night of drink, smoke and talk. And a most cherished time.

In the morning, we took our time, got coffees at the Tim-Hortons a stone-throw away from our spot by the road. Consistent traffic, but not busy, and after four hours from the night before, it was the longest we've waited. "Fucking people around here man, a lot of the old and grumpy or young and high-flown," I said. But that is where we invented our game: Road Nuts.

It started after throwing Brett's peanuts on the road and waiting for cars to crush them. He had a bag full. But then we added rules. We stood off the road and tossed a peanut between the road-lines, if it landed outside then you lost a point, like strokes in golf going negative and positive. If your peanut re-mained uncrushed for fifteen-minutes then you gained a point, but each peanut could only give three points and then it was removed from the game. Each player must have two in-play at a time and no more than three. Whoever scores higher once a set time to leave was reached or a ride came, wins.

Road Nuts passed the time like no other. There's a kooky hilarity in a peanut getting run over. It makes no sound and is left in a spot of dust. Our poor rest, booze and long travels, had us laughing unending as we sat in the stones and frowners passed by.

After another four ours at the spot that now had thirty-six dead peanuts, our ride was a young hip duo heading to Prince Edward Island: The average but slight hipster, Robin. And full-throttle, ripped-jeans, pierced-nose, leather-vest hippy, Jessica.

Brett and I got in the back of their Ford Focus, which offered great space despite the guitar that we kept safe between us. For the first while I was not sure if they were a couple, but both were fun and kindhearted. Jess was from Quebec. Robin was from L.A. but had been living in Quebec for seven years, studying music in hope to be a professional while he worked testing video games. Jess was a student. He was thirty-two, eight years older than her.

"Before we left," said Robin, "we were like, 'If we see any hitchhikers then we're picking them up.'" Then he put his hand on her thigh. So then I knew.

Jess controlled the tunes and played everything from pop to underground-grunge. On the way, we detoured to go on Hartland Bridge, the longest covered bridge in the world. Real fun. A five-hour trip from there, I slept for three, watched trees pass for two. Then we began the cruise along the bridge to P.E.I.

The Harland Bridge, longest in the world crossing ice-covered water. At least this wonder had a view. And it was beautiful all ways around as we drove from the sun setting down for us yellows and orange in a boundless away and eternal horizon that lulls in in its palm the ocean's lust.

Our first full day in P.E.I., we toured the town of Summerside. The boardwalk followed the sea to a trail ending in a circle by the shore where walkers looped and finished their route. But signs said the trail closed at night by ten-thirty, so we made our runs for groceries and booze then set camp in the circle. An ideal place and view, with a bench faced at sea, untouched grass for our feet and private beach, if we walked down the rock-ledge, which we did after having three drinks, then returned for more, back down again, each time measuring the rate of the tide sliding into and tracing its soul, to rest.

Another cherished night with many stars.

The next day, we strayed through the town, finding a used bookstore. Time to replace my lost book. I grabbed a copy of Fifth Business by Robertson Davis, and Brett roamed around because he still had much left of his book. So we laid by the shore and read for the day.

In Tim-Hortons for coffee and Wi-Fi, we planned out route out of the island. But after checking his account, Brett said he had far less money than expected and would have to head home early. He was pissed. And for strange reasons, it was good news to me, not of his misfortune, but that I could get along with my plan and settle into wherever I would be renting in Moonwake. A shortened trip meant scratching two places: Fundy, Cape Breton or Halifax. In accordance with money, fun, time and location, Halifax was where we would go.

That night, our last, we swung up our packs and ventured the road towards the exit, looking for a place to sleep. Only houses and small businesses, so we settled on the lot behind a bakery and laundry mat. Our tents to the back wall, the open land casting out from that side lent an ease to forget the world, routine and regular, that scurried its noise from the other.

In Brett's irritation and my anxious discomfort, we entered out talk with quarrelling tongues and minds. I don't remember who started what, what words or by whom they were spoken, but all true thoughts came out.

"What makes you think you are right, and how do you know for sure there that God exists," he said.

"I don't know for sure, but when I look at the evidence from history, which we have discussed, and the intelligence of the universe that science unveils, I can only answer its birth and keep by the hand of an all-powerful God. The fine-tuning of the cosmos must make one at least pose the question of intelligent design. And yes, with today's theories in metaphysics and a multi-verse, some say that there is no need for God's hand in creation, because in billions of solar-systems, within billions of galaxies, inside endless dimensions, there is bound to be the right conditions to create life. But this is leap of faith like no other. As the noted physicist, David Berlinski, who is agonist, says that quantum cosmology has yet to explain the birth or fine-tuning of the universe, so you see, there is no definite proof or disproof of God. Both sides must have faith."

"Well I don't believe in anything if I can't sure. I don't hold to a set of beliefs. I believe in what is," he said.

"But that's just being agnostic. Not holding to a religion doesn't mean you don't hold to a distinct worldview and particular set of values and truths. Even if it's not neatly laid out, everyone's worldview follows definable beliefs and ideas."

"Why does everything have to be named? I don't follow anything, there is no names or beliefs if you just don't care," he said.

After that, it was back and forth until he had enough.

"I'm going to bed, my head hurts and I'm pissed about my account, I'll see you tomorrow," he said.

In the morning, we packed and swung up packs by nine. On our hour way to the bridge, without standing or trying, our ride was a middle-aged family man happy as hell to help and he dropped us at the bridge.

We stood at our spot on the road just before the tolls. Car after car, all tourist and families. But in the hour our ride was two hags in their thirties, Amanda and Autumn. And we cruised along by mass and might of the ocean, into New Brunswick.

In the car we got high and had a roady. They had two cold beers left over from their apparent hell of an evening. These girls were beasty. Even Amanda referred to herself as a gnarling looking bitch, after a good party night, drugs, booze and boys (thumbs up to those fellas) they had no care in picking up two guys on the side of the road.

It was great. A ride, beer and firm high since it had been days after running out of sweet tea. They dropped us at the on-ramp to Halifax.

We opened our arms to the wind in our joy and flying skulls on the side of the road. For the first twenty-minutes we sat on our packs doing nothing. Faces passed bitchy and confused.

Our ride was a couple that looked misplaced together. The man was half Pilipino, clean-cut, thick and strong, and the woman looked older by at least a decade, fragile frame like an addict. For thirty dollars, they drove us to Halifax and dropped us downtown.

I arranged for our stay with a host named Joey.

His profile-photo was a handsome young man with nice clothes and money. And he came to pick us up in his good-as-new SUV, dress shirt tucked in tight-fitted dress pants, shined leather shoes and loud slicked back hair. But he conversed like courteous man of good character. His family held wealth, and it allowed him and his brother to start a trade-show company. So, at twenty-five, he was where most dreamed to be for the rest of their lives.

After settling us in his apartment he recommended places to eat, as he was to meet a friend then back up with us for a night on the town. So Brett and I stayed through the streets of the harbor-hung city. A city with thirst, endless young and steam-raw lapped nightlife.

After some drinks with his friend, who was a professional rower and near Olympian, Joey, Brett and I entered the night. Beginning with too many pitchers at a pool hall, my captivation and love for Joey sprout over beer and cue-smashing, us three arm-glomming howled in our shoulder-locked hoot. Then off to a pub.

And there I say among dancers, bashers, singers and skin-craved flames, them all the throng. All swallow mindless the next, and that, and that, instant of mind. I got a four-foot long blank receipt from the tender and whiskey-jotted the room:

★

Some spit-talk in ears, or grab at my wrist for attention, but are not just them all—they are sisters and brothers, along with whom-just-met, Joey.

As here we are, oh, and here we are, yes. Here we all are, toe-tappin' away in the city, with its grand-loosened horde, parading-smug cats, used-bare hussies, and skin-prowling pigs.

A cover band slanders its crowd as the tender diddles by with a glass balanced atop his head, and Joey shakes his tongue and winks at me. With this pen, on this paper, if can, I scavenge and claw any charm in this bar.

But it's all that I wanted.

So, fuck-of-me drink, oh eh, we are handed the night to be broken and proud. Everyone tries singing a song. All I wanted. But I'm strap-funneled a brew of hankered fond-flesh and a mock of my voice that surrounds me.

★

"Keep fucking going," said Brett, tossing his arms around me after his drunk-ramble through the bar. I finished both sides of one strip, and without request, the tender handed me more. Brett was gone, off to roam then appear beside me once done delving in waist-grooves and sways. Then a dickered chum pops-up beside me wet-grinned and lost, so tip-ding-tap low to his glass, hurrah with swig and cheers to our hell. Always tap low, because once I was told, that in China the height of your cheers is a gauge of respect, with a tap of your glass above others meaning you see them and their status beneath you.

Watching Brett make his way over, I went back in my mind to when we were in the bushes. To our time in the trees and coarse lands where bugs crawled without laws along on bodies. Our time, under the stars sitting in dirt with nothing to do. No regular, routine or plan. Time to drink far, howling the loudest, away from family and home. In the bushes we met, and in it is our pure accord that breathes and leads through the trees. As my brother comes, grabbing my pen and the paper, scribbling: *FOR THE DEAD.*

And we howled it out to the night, slamming our drinks as the liquor slid down our chins.

We left that bar.

We entered a new one. One with a more dancing music and chaos.

Regardless, a well-timed surprise that livened the night on our way to the club.

At entry, Joey took and lifted a petite whore who had ran to his arms.

"I got a lot side-chicks around here," he said.

It was the meat-womb of the city and our presence were the men set to bore, drool and moan. All around, brazen young men strut in cheap blazers and their stiff tinsel-hair. High and low, wet slender girls bent in skin-dresses and their ripened cream-hair. All claimed by the music shooting serrated-volts in their pores as come-dripping words slide inside ears and thick-thrust dogged in their privy-holes. When the drop of the music boomed, the tenders discounted their duties, and chose to clap *woohoo's* to the sounds. But I told one of them to give me a strip of receipt.

"How the fuck are you doing tonight," said the D.J., answered by *UUAAHHH's* and *WOUAARRGG's*. In the place— all I wanted—souls reached for another's something to feel something, but grinded teeth and scraped their eyes mad for the ever-forsaken-rouse to leave.

I shook in the corner exploring discontentment, deviation and decadence as I frothed to be inside a woman and knew I could be, by the gift of free-will. But right then I had only disgust, a pen, and two shots of liquor. I slugged both and whiskey-jotted:

★

A swung lay chorus of our gleamed-braided bodies standing in each other's holograph, and them all watching our faces staring opposed.

No one speaks—and ONE, two, three, ONE, two—at distance, just noise, see-through Adam and see-through Eve merged spotlit on stage flicker-clear. All eyes fixed, a few in the crowd bobbing, tapping and drinking the bass chords hoofed out of stadium speakers. The rest are gut-throated and still.

Standing in ourselves transparent-fused, I face left, you face right, both whispering, "We are the gods. We have control." ONE, two, three. Vruh. Vruh. Vruh. A silk-symphony licks up women from their seats, waist-bent swaying thirsty, and the men grunt gratified, ruling. Together we say, "God can go," as the speakers thunder the dome. A slow standing crowd. A slow stripping down. Vruh. Vruh. Vruh.

Zooming out: building.
Zooming out: dirt.
Zooming out: city.
Zooming out: earth.

Zooming out: space, stretched and untold, where God sits curious of a slight noise, maybe something, wailing out, "God, goodbye," from the thrash of our flesh trying and all saying bye, as Liege looks down, saying, "Alright," and nods to us—"Try."

★

Joey came over and introduced me to the whore, Skyler. She was attractive, but reeked of worn-skin. And she fucked-off in minutes to entertain some guys, seeming to have ties with them all. His slut, Joey told me, offering her, saying, "If you want her, she'll suck your dick, and if I say 'fuck my friend', she'll say 'okay'."

So after her whirl with the guys, she scurried over with a friend. We all giddied to a stall in the ladies room to whiff-up cocaine. Skyler rubbed up against me with no room to move, with her bare legs and ass on demand. We had our chops then ran out as women screeched cussing. I was zooming and on the ground. The plan was to fuck her.

Jittered, shaking and probing all moments with aim-less-flit eyes for any pleasure, eye-contact, body-praise, beer thieves, fight or relation. Bodies careened and wade in a stale carp stew. Creatures true to their need. I wanted truth in my need, so I let it all in.

At the end of the night, Skyler came back home with us. Joey passed out. Brett and I sat silent with Skyler and then some guys called her to go to a party. "You guys want to come?" she asked. So Brett and I followed her down the street to a house answered by young men who refused us our entry, but laughed as Skyler walked in. She gave her least sorry then turned away while a sneering man closed the door.

Brett and I looked at each other, then Skyler, and walked away.

We walked back to Joey's.

I knew I would leave alone.

The substance, misdeeds, and failure to have even a sin fulfilled, set off my need to flee.

"Fine, then go. Do it, but you'll regret it. Trust me, I've been in your exact place before," said Brett.

"I know, but I don't care. I just need to go," I said.

"And where are you going to go, it's three in the morning," said Brett.

After arguing for an hour, Brett went to bed and I began packing.

"Alright," I said, standing over him. "Goodbye, my brother."

"Ahw, fuck eh, you're actually doing it," he said. He sat up and embraced me. "We'll see each other when you come back at Christmas."

"Sounds good," I said. "Love you as ever, my brother."

Then I climbed out the window and trekked through the streets.

Travel did not speak with the same voice as it did from the common to foreign roads. And now, alone, from foreign to the next, travel spoke unknown words. I walked in the wrong direction so I could look to the sea. The water gave its voice, but not the same as the waters that flowed at home. Displeasing, the further along. I started for the road.

To the history, so often necessity, followed and repeated. I left the unknown to another crude demanding land yet walked by my feet and soul. And though nameless, always a voice. How it spoke along like it knew me, the choice, necessity and cost—my family, love and sense. An illusion, casting loss, heard by the water. Not from home, but still grave when stood by, as I blew smoke along the wind and walked away.

The involuntary line: keep moving.

PART IV

Humor Sleep, Pig

On a bus.

A drunk guy sat behind me, obnoxious and rude, oblivious to the fact that everyone around him wanted him to shut-the-fuck-up. But he seemed to like me.

He got off for a smoke when we arrived in Moonwake.

"You smoke weed?" he asked. "We got fifteen-minutes before the bus leaves."

"I'm not getting back on, this is my stop. But I'll have a hoot if you don't mind," I said.

We walked behind the building in my new city. He bickered about life, woman, men and money. A bi-sexual, I saw it once he told me. So I got my high and said farewell.

Picturing the map in my head, I walked to the nearest street which happened to be Main, and I took it all the way down as it lead to the road of my new home. I knocked on the door.

Gerry answered. "Hello there, Rive, come on in."

I had searched online for places to rent before Brett and I left for our travels. Gerry had a room for rent that was more than reasonably priced and centrally located.

He showed me around and told me his expectations: Here is recycling, which is on Thursdays; make sure the window in your room are shut all the way if you find it cold; use this cloth to wipe down the shower when you're done; these shelves are yours and so is the half of the fridge.

Gerry was an intelligent man, evident by his speech and rambling. A recent retiree from his career at the company for thirty-two years. He didn't own a car because everything was within walking distance. An avid baseball fan and consumed with the game of bridge. His post-work life consisted of bridge class and umpiring twice a week. He went to the pub on the weekends and saw old friends every two weeks.

My first night, trying to find a bar, I stopped in a pub with long-sitters, people eating on dates, and no talk or fun. Everyone dressed formal. Beer was seven bucks. I had one and asked if there was a place in town to play pool.

The tender said, "Well, if you don't mind something ghetto, there's a place called Saned Men, down the road."

So I made my way and entered the mother of dives.

Karaoke and chaos ran rapid. There was a small *L* shape bar in the corner, five slot machines in the back, fifteen-by-five stage along the barred-window-wall, and beaten-up pool table in the center of a family of hooligans. But they were forthright and happy-as-hell. I got a beer for two-fifty and went making friends, beginning each meeting with my previous month's adventure to impress and gain interest. One guy, dickered by eight-thirty, both arms sleeved with wild-beasts, wearing a jean-vest and fedora, had no problem talking to strangers, as he dally-eyed me up and down, nibbling his lip, asked if I was gay.

"I'm not gay though," he said. "I'm bi-sexual."

"No, my brother, I'm not gay. I have a girlfriend," I said.

"Doesn't mean anything. Lots of gay guys date girls. You sure you're not gay?"

"I can tell you without a doubt that I'm one-hundred-percent straight. Sorry, man," I said, patting his shoulder. My first discomfort ended at that.

Outside for a smoke, an obvious character bumbled about. Not a big guy but seemed insane. A jittery fellah, always talking and cracking jokes. We chummed around, and then he threw out a mention of him being gay, but said he was joking.

"A lot of gays here though, in Moonwake," he said. "I'm Tommy, by the way."

When I went inside to piss, the man in a jean-jacket shouted behind me. "You got a nice looking penis." All I could do was laugh and say, "Oh, fucking eh." Because he meant no harm and was liquored-up good.

Tommy ran on the stage slamming his head in the air as he sang, great voice and on key. After his song, he ran and wrapped his arm around me wailing nonsense. Hell of a guy.

And so I was emerged, walking inside the relevant people's waters under fire of their thought. They moved too fast, not talking timed or relevant, and it took my toes long to touch down to their holy dirt. As a proud man kept stroking his inked arms, and a quiet gal took her second look, definitely in my eyes.

But I did nothing.

Outside for another smoke, under my new skies that had calloused in blue over those of the east, which on that night included me. I waited for black and the stars.

And I wanted to leave—to roam starved and fed on thought as the loonies swished another drink laughing out air from the depths of what should have all been relevant. The quiet gal looked in a third time, as I wanted to leave, and did nothing but finish my drink and ask for another.

Then I met Finnegan.

Eighty-two years old. A regular of thirty-years, sitting stone-faced alone at a table, our friendship began with the booze-loosened me plopping in the seat beside him.

"How's it going?" I said.

"Oh fuck, stuck in this shit-hole again." His bottom lip shook steady.

After our names, background and recent affairs, we talked about life doomed to a bar.

"You ever seen the movie Barfly?" he said.

I laughed because Bukowski was one of my favorite poets. I told him of my reason to be in town which was to write my first book of poetry. He pursed his lips a lot, never showing much interest or care. He stood a small distance away and alone from the crowd when he smoked. He spoke to himself aloud, old-timer grumbles, like: "Oh, what a joke."; "Eh, this place?"; "Ah fuck, these people don't make any sense." I would listen and walk over as he was already creeping towards me. I knew we were pals.

Then I met Tyler.

On that same first night, Tyler and I talked for a half-hour outside on a cub about Saned Men, the city, drugs and jail. He had done time for selling the hard stuff and had smartened up after having a kid. But he still dealt. And so came my chance to get the drug I had been eager to try:

Speed.

It was clear that he'd had one hell of a life in all the sad and painful ways. Once sure of the fact that I wasn't a nark, he handed me a pill and gave me his number. Then I asked for two more.

When I walked back into the bar, Finnegan was doing karaoke. He sang "The Wreck of the Edmund Fitzgerald" by Gordon Lightfoot. Finnegan stood stiff on stage, beer in hand, delving the tune with the whole of soul. I took a shot of whiskey and cherished this time.

After Finnegan's song, I wasted no time walking back to the room of my new home.

The streets were cold. Wind thrashed, cars scurried, drunks rambled, bums quivered and grumbled for change.

I dashed through the foreign streets and staggered to Gerry's front door.

I creeped up the stairs to my room. I opened my laptop on the tiny coffee-table.

I took all three pills of speed.

I fashioned lines of coke along a book and zipped two up into me. I gagged, reaching for a bottle of whiskey under the bed.

I was in my new home. A box.

My body pulsated—fierce. My mind digested rich paths of thought—new—birthing like strikes of lightning—enthralling. My soul submerged into the All that consumed reality--

Bringing the Saned Men family and spell along with me. In my body of scum-sweat, for twenty-eight hours without leaving my chair, wired to zeal, high on a legion of drugs, jazzing-forth on the job, I whiskey-jotted.

★

Here.

Now—I speak to you.

We meet in the present of our conversation.

This is now for both of us.

I had begun speaking to myself (and you)—blazing through memories and thoughts—for the past three hours since returning from Saned Men this evening. Searching my thoughts, memories, and recent exploration of new lands and my soul.

Searching for Him.

I began our conversation, and now I will bring it to a close.

So, do you have a five-year plan?

I had one and now I sit by a window in an unknown world, far from family, friends, and all that is familiar.

★

(1:47 a.m.):

These blankets, wool, itch.

No smooth around—no stars, counted five.

These bricks that my forest-feet walk on are storied, speaking.

Well, depends on the street, because when I tried to get a drink

In a fine-man requested place, I found utter dread.

So, I went where the tender said, "But it's ghetto."

And oh, these people here east, our land, will tell you things.

Giving all and enough to send you back to their stories

Through their own dirt-bruised fuckin feet.

Where a father throws his son through the ice,

To sink or become a man.

And I am sent back with these gifts: pills, powder, and stories.

I lie in a foreign bed, in wool sheets, but have silk in my blood.

From a gift, a pill, making me glad, although it is what ruined

Many of my new vagabond brothers and sisters.

I had sat with the stars weeks ago, on a river, counted five shooting.

But these skies sleep void of the galaxy's grace.

City lights decay the heavens.

I now commune with the teeth-grinding, devilry-seeking—
authentic freaks.

The soul-grunting, joy-hollering—spirit gifts.

In a lawless bar—down the street from the combed-hair
folk

Who requested, but warned, going to.

The bar—a home for the Freak Gifts.

A home for me.

A place where—when I first entered—a near naked man
thrashed on stage

Screaming someone's song into a mic—to a drinking,
fighting, dancing,

Mourning, hiding, worshipping family—living dust.

They are not known—so they cannot be forgotten.

But here I am, cuddled, kept and bitter, because I wanted
the skin

Of some white-teeth-cloud-strollers that remind me of
you.

You, my dear—dead and lost Love.

I am alone.

I miss your skin.

But I have a gift:

Molasses-grinned, jolting me down to sleep, in wool.

I itch alone—so far away.

★

I have a room on the edge of a river.

Gerry let me use a small coffee-table as a desk. It's large
enough to fit my laptop and a bottle of whiskey. It faces out
the window towards the river. This is where I will be writing.

Here the reflection of the sun comes through to my eyes. Rays seep through the glass into my box. This box is my new home for the next while.

For the first week I stayed in my room a lot, smoking weed, sketching images, reading things online, drinking coffee, drinking alcohol and deteriorating in my head over thoughts of her. But I also made my way out of the house to rejoin with humanity. I would go to coffee shops, book stores, the library, and Saned Men. This would allow me to think of things, do my drugs with thought, and observe the picture around me.

I sit at my tiny coffee-table all day and night, watching and listening to the outside world. The buildings were beautiful and large, with purity in the day and glorification in the night. Humming of voices, the traffic if close, cheering, laughing, dining, roaring, booming, and everything that a civilization sounds when it moves, engages and consumes: This was a place, a city, an attraction, an industry, a history, a life.

For the first week I've been a sloth, suffering in my pity. Reminders filled: I am alone, she is gone, abandonment kills, and you are in love. What I needed was to create something beautiful containing all that I was, into something visible. Yes, that is what I thought, I am a poet, and that is what I will do. So, I searched for the life that I was prepared for in this lustrous land.

For three months I will be here.

I measured my room. It is a perfect square, ten-by-ten. I have my one bag: a 70L hiking pack. The more things—the more distractions. So I packed light: minimal clothes, toothbrush, books, cigarettes, matches, beef jerky, and a laptop. I am always on my laptop: watching videos about politics, government affairs. I am always listening to music. When I am high, I watch conspiracy videos about September 11th, the war in the Middle East, and the New World Order.

To begin my day today, the toast is not going, because I never get it going. I don't like toast much. I don't like eating much in general most of the time. My eating patterns are not good because I sleep so late, drinking all night, reading and studying things, trying to create something of value.

When I wake up, I do not want food, although my stomach is burning, I do not want food. What I want is a substance to get my mind out and able to live in that particular day, with the things that it brings, the people, smells, weather and tasks. I do not like tasks. When I wake up I want to smoke pot and drink, have a cigarette, listen to music.

There are of course the days when I have work to do. Work. Since I was young I've worked all kinds of jobs, factories, golf courses, markets, family camps, churches, call centers and even planting trees. I have done things, but I have always relied on the support of my parents. Not so much moral support, or much of wisdom and social living. I have been supported with money. A currency that gives me food, cleans my teeth, takes me places, allows leisure activities, and replaces the necessities. But words like *necessity* are relative. A car may be a necessity for some, but to others, a luxury. And this has been spewed out before.

Spewed. Information being spewed and reiterated, repeatedly. And remember, repetition, could be, may be, to some and in some way, insanity.

So, we've all been spewing things. When I was boy, the age of ten let's say, I was told I needed to do my school work to do well in school, because I needed a good job. All that was on my mind were action heroes, stories, movies, books, characters and adventures. I loved adventures and that is a major reason why I am here today.

My mother, she has helped me with many things. All the things in relation to physical needs, the bottom of Maslow's triangle. This is good. It is important to have the bottom fulfilled so that ascension can occur. But that is the most that I have got from her. *I love her though*, as they say, I should say—and not that I don't, but it not that simple. Sometimes it is more of a pity than a love. I love the things she has done for our family and how she has provided, but I do not care much for her ridiculous claims, mindless worry, strangled judgment and social unawareness. It took twenty-six years to get out of my home.

My father is a good man. A small business owner and hard working. He follows politics and has theories on *what really happened*, and the *They*. At this point, my parents are irrelevant. They are ways away, vacationing and enjoying their time in retirement. Mother, bless her, sends me money when I need it. And yes, it is often.

I began walking in the mornings. It is gorgeous here in the mornings. Today, I exit my room to the back porch. There are some shrubs in the way and people walking about to all the things offered. To save time, I hop over the railing, through the mulch and shrubs right into the middle of traffic.

I enter a breakfast diner.

At the diner there are more than forty people inside and on the patio. They sat me on the patio close to the entrance. To my left are many open tables and a few families enjoying their breakfast. To my right are more tables and a family, couples, teenagers, and seniors. I am alone in a way, facing out onto the river, with open left and open right.

I take out my notebook with reluctance and fear. What was beautiful and significant about this scenery? What about the blue, and what about the symmetry? What about the converging point and what about the texture? Are these things good? My pencil sketched it all and it was good.

I have sketched dozens of sceneries. They do nothing for me. I think they are beautiful but they capture nothing more than land and trees. Although, each image is unique, and they are indeed pleasurable to the eye. But what about the people to my left and right?

Halfway through my lukewarm, syrup-soaked blueberry waffle, I had sketched the left of the distant island and the right. I had sketched the sky, the mountains, the ripples and the curves. But the people left and right have eaten and left. I could have captured the couple laughing to a cheers of their full day ahead. I could have captured the young friends, making jokes, discussing woman, discussing man, discussing vulgar beauty and discussing me. I could hear them under themselves saying things about my posture and my surrounding—I was alone. I heard them speak about my sketches—that they could not see—as their jokes consisted of a literal nothing, disguised, cloaked in humor: "Look at that guy drawing."

Is my waffle interesting? Does my waffle mean anything? I could have captured this waffle and maybe it would mean something. I could have shown those people's faces with the scenery behind them above, but with darkness and hell below. I can do anything I want.

★

Why am I speaking to you? I am speaking to you so you can do the thing that is best for you in the present moment of your reality. What is your reality? The question appears simple enough.

The house I rent from is perfect, with all the things I want. It has a stove, so I can make food, and a sink where I can wash things. There is enough space for a couch and a desk. All I need is a couch and a desk. There are things I need to do today, but myself will not let me. A picture must be made that can tell the things within my reality, the seemingly invaluable, and finite euphoria from substances. It must be shown. Can it be shown?

I am going to look at the clouds above me so that they can give their sense of belonging to me. Good things in life, pleasures of all sorts, are supposed to keep us going: saliva, meat, cheese, liquids, sights, sounds, greens, yellows, are all supposed to keep us going.

My left hand radiates, it has the sun on it. I look at my pack. There is my pack that will unload a soul. It will unload a lonely horrid soul.

My love is gone, all of it. Deception took her, that hideous scum.

Whiskey.

Retrieve the whiskey from the bag now. Open those blinds as large as you can. Look at that—look at the shimmer along the waters. Window: the entrance to other real things outside, outside of my thoughts and senses, until now. Now look at that—the shimmer along the water is here for me.

The drink will help remove the aching memories. What I had. When I had. What I knew. What I saw. I saw the breaths. I saw the skin and softs in all the true places, moving as they do, when lovers unite.

It has been years since I lost her, and now I am away in a new place, afraid. But there is so much joy within, because I know of all the possibilities. I can learn so much here with all the different things a city has to offer.

Responsibilities are important but I also need experiences. I am going to find a beautiful woman and make life something important for us, together, regardless of where it leads, and it will be fulfilling.

But now, I create.

I can drink as much as I want and need.

And I've stocked up on drugs.

So now, this whisky. Turn on the songs that have been giving me a reason to keep a smile and crave creation. Craving creation, as pathetic and delusional as it can be, has potential to be valuable and beautiful. Create it. Turning on the songs, I look out the window and I know I am alone and degrading.

At age twenty-six, I am degrading. My teeth, they are disgusting and I have had seven fillings and two root canals. My hair is nice.

I do a line of coke. Yes, for the memory and creation.

Yes, my hair.

My hair is nice. Greasy most of the days because, although I shower daily, I do not wash bi-daily. When I shower, I masturbate and stand still for fifteen minutes under scorching water. My hair has grown too long, but most think it is handsome on my face. When I look at my face, it is thin, but also handsome. My diet and sleeping schedule is horrid. Although I am underweight, I have a strong tight core and a bit of muscle.

I will begin eating right and sleeping better now that I am here. Look at everyone out there. Such a warm and perfect day with everyone walking to get food or sight, smiling with the most important humans to them, due to relation, relevancy, or fulfilment.

I am going take a nap though. Close the blinds as tight as they can, and then get up around eight when it is dark. The night is time for drugs and creation. I am going to write something important. I will make something to show what my soul is under sight, feels within a grasp, tastes in a kiss, and sounds as it is inflicted with wounds. That is what will be put onto paper.

When do I begin work this week? I must begin within three days. I need to do that.

So I will nap and then do drugs and write. My dreams will be vivid of her.

Freedom. I am also in a place of freedom. Money. I barely have enough for my stay here. I am enraged and worn by my defect of constant comparing—my life to the lives of other humans. There are many people who still rely on their parents for money, even in their thirties. And I am not relying on them for much, just survival.

Money, the root of all things, but what is it? It's more momentous than just a currency, physical or otherwise. It is, like everything apart from nature, a man made creation from the sources of nature. It is an idea, represented by a physical object. It is an idea of worth, value, quality and quantity. It is the fundamental thing to get—to get other things.

It is a god.

It is universal.

It is the commanding order.

A universal thing that could lead a man to put a bullet in women's chest so he can take an object, called a purse, to get to the object, called a wallet, to get the fundamental object—money.

It is the commanding order that can rule one's soul.

It is the root of our Vile Hour—in a world's heap of retching breaths.

I need to go to the bar. It is almost eight o'clock.

To Saned Men!

★

(9:37 p.m.):

From the eyes of God:

Rive, rocking to the thought of insanity, accepted what was to come. There were drinks to be had, and scoffs: oh, the scoffs for his pity will echo tonight. No pretty girls could be found in this bar, in this city.

Bodies too well clothed had him surrounded. Fools, he thought, obnoxious and ungrateful. Worse things were happening than what these people were wining about. Perfect hair glistened so commercial, smack-pucker red lips on young beauties serving, new jeans tight-up-the-ass pretty customers, well-jeweled and blazer business folk. A woman with her perfect hair and clunking heels as she struts her presumably well used body to the restroom, where she stares at herself long minutes upon exiting. Her phone, why does she need to stare at her phone, looking at pictures of frivolous moments from the lives of her foolish friends? Vanity.

Rive knew that he got this way when something did not go his way. These people have their own problems, and some of them might be thinking the same towards him. The way he sat, slouched, could be seen as arrogant.

"Fuck off," he muttered to them all.

He needs more to drink. Of course, he knows it will set off the path, but it seems necessary now, doesn't it? Rive flung two fingers along the air at the young tender.

"You're having one of those nights?" said the tender, laughing with pity.

Another whiskey came. Wonderful.

The T.V was beginning to have that special effect on him—surreal beauty of immerging time and space: that existence was and is forever being, apart from the eyes observing a screen. Five whiskeys. Now Rive read minds, or at least tried. Like his father, he taunts with realms doubted but believed in. It's not reading minds, rather placing thoughts and actions in people's heads.

Fine, there's one pretty women, thought Rive. The woman wore soft linen, a smooth beige skirt, dark leggings and slip-on shoes. Her hair, dark with golden streaks, and her skin, clear. A bit of makeup, not too much, and her teeth, intact. Nose is funk. But her eyes—they are there. Her eyes. Come here, thought Rive. Look at her eyes. Those eyes are emeralds pits. A deadly fall but glorious. A large man, wearing a jean jacket that didn't suit him, sat beside the woman. Is she with him? Come here. Leave that guy. Come, and sit beside Rive.

Cell phone vibrating. Alright, ten bucks it is Mother. Ten bucks anyone? Tender? Ten bucks, you guys over there, you family, that guy, those kids, ten bucks? Rive cracked his knuckles as he pulled out his phone. Text: *Riven. Where are you? It's been over a month and you have not returned my call.*

"I think I'll sit with you," said the woman who was told to through the mind.

"Because you heard me in your head?" said Rive, without choking on a swallow of whiskey.

"What?" asked the woman, still smiling. "No, I saw your jacket. You're from Toronto?"

"No. Where are you from?" asked Rive.

"Here. But I'm leaving for Halifax tonight for my father's birthday," said the women, smiling, facing, leaning.

"Interesting."

"Yes. My father is not doing well. It will be a wonderful family surprise for him to see us all."

Rive mushed his lips and dipped his head.

"Oh, no doubt," said Rive—the polite gesture of not-giving-a-fuck, but wanting to prevent a bit more madness by assuring another human they are spot-on: The Western world lives like that—talks, moves, sighs, breathes like that.

"My brother will be there, which is great, because he hates these kind of things. And my cousins, finally! Oh, and my aunt, whom I just adore. The in-laws are coming, so that will be a riot. You know what I mean? Oh, family drama, family drama. Just another episode!" said the pretty woman.

"Episodes!" Rive tipped two chair legs off the floor. "Fucking tell me about episodes."

The woman's smile grew. "Can I buy you another?" Her hand moved to Rive's drink, brushing his arm.

Rive's shoulders had relaxed into their normal shape, hunched, elbows propped, head leaning forward and tilted to the right. His eyes prowled up to his brows, beneath dark greased bangs, glaring at the mouth of the woman.

"I don't drink," he said.

He tossed back his head, letting whiskey slide down into him. He slammed the glass—seven whiskeys—watching the woman's mouth droop into hell. She tensed and frowned.

Rive slid off the bar, bumped into three chairs, and walked away with a giggle.

★

(2:56 a.m.):

This is it.

I came home from Saned Men after thirteen drinks and a pocket full of pills.

I want to finish my journey of creation. I want to leave behind a gift of thought. But all of that may be gag-worthy. Truly, I have spoken garble and wallowing filth. But I crave further rage. You can hear it.

Friend, brother, sister—my goal here is hope. I ache for all whimpering voices—as my voice is among them. I taste the sorrow beneath the eyes of those that have not seen the light in too long—as my eyes are adrift in darkness.

But this I know:

YOU—CAN—BREAK—FREE.

★

(3:29 a.m.):

I gag on the truth. On the good kept close. The holding of my hands on pills of escape. Escape from reality's affliction: a flight from existence. On a way to the always, has to be, consequence. The bone-slither, sat in taunt of me, held the most near and close that can be without a swallow. It slides in my ear with the truth that I deserve this torment and more. For refusing all and any good to enter my being. That is why I gag, held close to a swallow.

So that is what I do. And then call for good to come back, if it will be had by my side again. And it came to me right then, almost near enough for me to reach and hold. But I gag to all that it is. Now held in my hand again—Escape—I curse that it be sent to hell, for its own ears to be slithered. But I fly from existence. And there will be no consequence, I say.

Keep far away, truth and good. I have what will solve this, the scum-skin, with more scum-skin. But for it to be had, it has to get in, without a gag. But it will go in now. Yes, this is my time I get my solve.

But I had sent me to hell to gag.

There is scum on my tongue but not in me. And water went in me the most simple and sad truth that it can. My Solve held wet in my hand.

Pills.

Gifts.

Try of my bones, soon again.

A swallow.

I gag.

PART V

A Coast

(5:21 a.m.):

Do you hear us? Our plea:

Just take us mad, leave us poor, or imprison us even in an endless Grudge-Line without room, kept as close to suffocation but never. At least give us a home, if you are going to take away everything. I know, we were wrong and not accountable, or concerned with You, Justice, but we did wonder a few times, of the time and day you would come for us. But here now, and not to have us caged, or held haunted and dragged in chains together with our qualms (since even they began to rot and do nothing). You come to us now, because of the inevitable time. You hold the eternal plan safe in your hand, not offering a choice of what our fate is or could be. Only the script, which reads the must. I know you have opened it, Ready to read soon, all that will be done to us when you declare. So we must prepare, God knows what will tear in and out of our Minds, or will purge out of teeth by the grins, leaving our faces. I know, you are out of grace and options, so must bring to us our Due, but can you hear bellowed-moans, under this sky you are bashing? Leave us be, we repent, stop hollering.

We are not dogs.

But you answer with lashes on our skulls:

Brutes. Deranged. Tell me. Can dividing the earth, behind the walls for only your suited, as you rape bare the poor, be ignored? Tell me! Answer. Testify and try to speak of grounded. Speak again of learned. You know nothing. I hear mumbled sniffing apes. Dust. The next jest of bones, the rot, creatures without purpose, left gnawed by its kind.

So to that, we weep:

All our bones are being broken. All souls are pouring into your flood, put away, held dunked, beneath your slamming sky, and you watch. The hammer of our heads. But there is no more mercy in your eyes.

And to that, you plunge a fist:

Too long, not knowing your thoughtless breath is a gift, only aware if reminded by the poor, threatened, afraid to lose any of your cheer. So take this breath and prepare for this kiss, a goodbye to your kind on each calloused lip, in all sorrowed-eyes, then tilt back your head. Hold that breath, to be impaled with truth, the place of your stature. Tongue-out for drips of any comfort, waiting for what never comes. Of you, I make statues of nothing, in a wait for the absent last drop.

Now we beg, hear our teeth scraping mad, and cries of the many:

All wake, there is a roar from the towns nearby, out red lives in fury, drummed to a march of their hate, beating with the ripples of flame. They trudge through the marsh at speed, repeating curse and swear to end our blood. And it is too late. We have only the lies of hope. So go. Sing and hum songs to your young, away from the window. Remember that sooth, as a child, the tune and voice of your mother. Fight now, for hope and sane, since time is a slow crawling slave as all of our dread has been tied to its back. Scavenge any thought that frees you of blame from the nearing chant, and shaking ground. Do not look out, the flames grow with speed, and will soon be here.

So go, Stay with your loved, and keep them away from the window. Sit, learn each charm of their face, then let the rest of your love run out and into the daughters, sons, and spouses, held tight in your arms. Do not stop your songs, no one will, even when jaws are clamped by the force of our thoughts of our state and what we have done. The thought, soon to be thrust into us and ripped through. A distraction from the kill, and most lethal thought, that many now hold a child who will die, soon, never to grow, stripped of the chance to have love, or hold their own. The flames are here. We bleed. Soon to end.

We see:

Our bones gash by the hate, and our heads thrash in your flood. But surged, still breathing, we seethe at your name, now known.

Do you hear us? Our curse:

You declared yourself to us, in the flood of an army, through them who will not, can never be just. They are human, but you sent them to judge, punish and bring us our due, though we have begged and confessed our faults. You will not relent, but come here declaring yourself true, slandering our souls, under dark-skies and blood-shed. We know now, and seethe at your name, the truth of what you are. Your spirit, hideous, and soul, gruesome, foul, hypocrite, liar, scum. You tried to pass-off the name and deeds of true Justice. Laughable filth. You send dirt, to tell dirt to be cleansed. At least we can see our fall. We divided land, but you take ours, we built walls, but you give power to those who are tearing them down in your name. And they will build new ones. The same as ours that you damned us for. We raped bare the poor, but you throw our women onto the streets, disgracing us, smacking and spitting at our faces, forcing yourself on top of our young, whispering horrid words. You are not Justice, but jeweled and declared by most to be, since you hold their heads drowned in your flood of hate, cursed skies and evil, seduced to be blind to your grip on their necks and their actions, like ours, but of far graver evil. Yet you tell them that they are pure, and deem their crimes as moral-rights, sent against us in your false-name, assured they are good and right, serving the truth, to plunder. While we are on our knees assured also, not of our value or good, but of our wrongs and deserving, destruction, in your false-name of Justice.

Do you hear your suffering, as you set to flame? We watch:

You held our heads in your flood of deception, to loathe and hate ourselves, waiting for drops of comfort. Statues unable to move. You led and let them take everything, for the cycle of confusion and decay to remain, so that you, Deception, have a purpose. But you are alone, smut in a mask, and true Justice will come. While you come mindless and lashing our young, by the hands of your puppets in your false-name, but their time will come. To have everything taken away. Then you will see your failure and strings, strung-up too, the puppet of no purpose but serving The Keeper of Truth. Your deeds have only ever been a tool of its will, hearing our plea, true Justice comes, so we will take our due and drown in cheer as we curse all you are, Deception. Damning your claim to be sovereign over our heads, now free, bled out below our sky, not holding a breath or saying goodbye, we wait for nothing. As all has come, our sinking statues of your head bent back and impaled by truth, to our end unseen, in the depths, grinning all the way down. Now do you hear us? You ape. Tell me, Deception, as you mumble and rot to dust. Do you hear each child of God gnaw on the jest of your bones? Hear our laughter.

Try speaking again and wait tongue-out. You dog.

Burn in hell.

★

(6:57 a.m.):

I took too many drugs, so I have to leave a note:

My heart rate is at a death speed that has me rag-dolled to the floor waiting to survive. Grabbing at any good thoughts in the ceiling fan, it's been fifteen minutes. A finger knocking the knuckle every two seconds, sometimes the nail, for my melody on the table leg, which is a wood and a solid, so I can touch it and feel it to keep me in this world. But the five options of my body are stirring into one and only giving, what I call Me, one thought, of a Me and the love for life, or the fear of dust. Knowing it will be slow and rich of pain and fear when death eats its meal without praying first—even it is not thankful and does not understand.

All the real that a five can give. How much with more. And what is the real for a Me of only atoms and the tiniest? I can't see the waves of light and voices. I can't taste a sad or smell a thought, but to a Me they must be a clear real with actual force and full of distinct marks, place-able on a Me or the others. Or at least all that I do is bound to the belief of their existence without question. Like not putting my hand in fire. That choice is made without thought or doubt that it was the right decision. The trust of a Me is in this, and every atom in it all, to their designs, tending in an orbit of foundational-force.

In the food I eat. Mouth I chew. Stomach I fill. Hands I do.

All atoms and all energy.

My lips, your hair, our kiss, every cell feeling it. My care for a You and all those thoughts, memories, tears, colors. Only atoms. And they are at war, imprisoning and imposing giant wills on the ones they can, and a Me thinks that it can know this and notice, but I can't, not with only five. I need more. Because drugs can't give even close to another. Just a real tempt of a new, and so soon to end, to an even more real starve. Just a me, doing things, swatting, sniffing, holding, swallowing a bunch of things, scattered with no time to know that this is a tiny all, inside an all that a Me would be left ragged-up drooling if put inside. This must and is a true full-real.

In a unified stand-alone-worthy. It kisses, it misses, it hates. Unseen, unknown, being crushed, burned, breathed, boiled. A war where all die but wait to return, changed and adjusted. A Must Be, an Is, an Always Will that has no true death, only killed in the form then invents the vison it chooses to control. A thing, which to a Me is the only real thing seen and known. But they must fall in love as they wait to expire with a quick kiss goodbye and tilt of a hat turning to continue on strolling down their path whistling their favorite tunes.

To an instant-birthed reunion.

Right now, and now, and now.

I knock, I knock, and I knock.

My pulse is not slowing down and if there is a God then I was warned by him last night when my heart flooded real at death speed. So you may be reading this, and I am dead, if that is the case, then that is fair and favorable.

Because I will tip my hat and turn away.

To continue down my path whistling my favorite tunes.

So do not grieve or care.

Cheerio, adieu and adieu.

I am soon to understand.

THE END

About the Author

N.C. Robert has a Master of Theological Studies. His schooling and general interest has always been in theology, philosophy and literature. He began writing poetry in high school and had his first poem published in Poetry Quarterly in 2013 titled "Resting Home." After that, he was inspired to write his first novel – A Coast.

www.ingramcontent.com/pod-product-compliance
Lightning Source LLC
Chambersburg PA
CBHW032227080426
42735CB00008B/754